# BUILDING COOPERATIVE PROCESSING APPLICATIONS USING SAA

John Tibbetts    Barbara Bernstein

John Wiley & Sons, Inc.

New York • Chichester • Brisbane • Toronto • Singapore

Tibbetts, John, 1946-
    Building cooperative processing applications using SAA / John Tibbetts, Barbara Bernstein.
        p. cm.
    Includes bibliographical references and index.
    ISBN 0-471-55485-5 (paper)
    1. IBM Systems Application Architecture.   I. Bernstein, Barbara.
II. Title
QA76.9.A73T53   1992                                          91-47989
004'.36—dc20                                                      CIP

Printed in the United States of America

10 9 8 7 6 5 4 3 2 1

for
**Gertrude Bernstein**
and
**Lillia Tibbetts**

Having lived through nearly all this century's astonishments, they remain intrigued and hopeful about the future.

# Contents

## III.   Distributed Design Models

# List of Illustrations

# *Foreword*

As we move toward the turn of the century, the search for improvements in productivity continues. The focus of this search has turned toward the desktop and the knowledge worker. Rapid advances in computer hardware and communication technology have provided exceptional opportunities for productivity tools on the desktop through the emergence of very powerful computer workstations and the increased capacity and cost/performance in computer networks. The key to the exploitation of these advances lies in the linkage between these new desktop workstations and the host networks.

The nontrivial task of constructing these cooperative processing linkages is made easier with the right help. This book by John Tibbetts and Barbara Bernstein is just that! The book offers its readers an opportunity to gain new expertise in the use of state-of-the-art computer hardware and software technology in order to add cooperative processing applications to today's leading-edge, open-distributed systems environments.

IBM and its software partners have been working hard to facilitate expanded use of cooperative processing by bringing SAA, AIX, new application development tools, and new cooperative processing applications to the marketplace. It has been my pleasure to work closely with John Tibbetts as he played a key role in analyzing and validating the concepts behind this effort and as he provided the technical development leadership that allowed one of our partners to implement advanced cooperative processing applications. In addition, John and Barbara's classes on "Cooperative Architecture and Design" have helped many gain the knowledge needed to begin to provide the productivity aids that this technology can bring.

In writing *Building Cooperative Processing Applications Using SAA*, John and Barbara have performed a service to the data processing industry, software vendor providers, information systems managers and specialists, the knowledge workers who use computers, and the companies that can benefit from cooperative processing. Everyone with an interest in cooperative processing can benefit from reading it.

> Earl Wheeler
> IBM Senior Vice President and
>    General Manager
> Programming Systems
> IBM Corporation
> Somers, N.Y.

# *About The Authors*

John Tibbetts is one of a handful of developers who have actually built working SAA applications. The system he designed, Tesseract Corporation's HRMS Intuition, has been in use at customer sites for over 2 years. He consults regularly with software vendors, large end users, and various labs at IBM, including the architects of Systems Application Architecture. He has worked with the Open Software Foundation on user interfaces and has served on the IBM task force on object-oriented programming. Tibbetts speaks widely at industry conferences and user group meetings, ranging from SHARE and GUIDE to the ICP Million Dollar Awards. He also made the keynote address at the 1991 OOPSLA conference.

John Tibbetts has been linking mainframes with PCs throughout his career. In 1981 he founded the first company devoted to using microcomputers as data workstations. Prior to that, he co-founded a company specializing in installing minicomputer-based timesharing systems for data management applications. He began his career at Tymshare. He holds degrees in philosophy and engineering from St. Louis University and Loyola University.

Barbara Bernstein has served as Managing Editor of the *SAA Update* newsletter. She and John Tibbetts write a column for *Strategic Systems*, and the quarterly "SAA Blueprint" series for *Software Magazine*, and they contribute frequently to other industry publications. She graduated from the University of Chicago and spent a number of years writing television commercials before turning to technical writing.

# Introduction

Since we first thought of writing this book, the Berlin Wall has fallen, apartheid in South Africa has begun unravelling, and IBM has formed an alliance with Apple. This gives us hope that cooperative processing—the bringing together of the PC and the mainframe worlds into a single-minded and even cordial whole—is not beyond the realm of possibility.

"Cooperative processing" is one of those terms that gets bandied about, praised and debunked, but not often understood. We hope in this book to sharpen up much ill-founded discussion. Cooperative processing is something specific, appropriate to many situations, tangible (in an increasing number of successful applications), and achievable by any motivated development team. It is also, we believe and will try to demonstrate, a good idea.

Management-oriented observers have written extensively about the crisis in commercial information systems. The problems that face computing are well known—massive backlogs, intractable incompatibilities, system integration nightmares, all of which are exacerbated by a paralyzing standoff between information systems (I/S) department traditionalists and personal computer/local area network (PC/LAN) upstarts. Cooperative processing could go a long way toward providing a solution in the form of powerful, flexible integrated new systems. Such systems have become a belated agenda of IBM's Systems Application Architecture (SAA) and similar architectural initiatives from other vendors and industry bodies.

## An Alternative to "Downsizing"

We write at a time when the press and many vendors are promoting a concept called "downsizing," by which they mean replacing mainframes with vastly more economical networks of PCs. This is a seductive but, in our opinion, simple-minded idea, like abolishing the federal government because local rule will be more efficient and democratic. Despite reservations about big government, we still believe that certain large-scale jobs can only be handled at a high and centralized level. So we want to stand up here for the continuing importance of centralized computing, whether on a mainframe, midrange, or minicomputer.

Certainly these machines' monopoly on computing power has vanished. Many jobs that mainframes once did (often poorly) are in the process of moving down to the LAN or individual PC level. But just because the locks have been opened and the water is rushing from the higher side to the lower does not mean that all the water will end up on the lower side. Eventually, "glass house" power and PC-user power will reach a stasis. Cooperative processing will provide one powerful way for mainframes and PC networks to establish a sort of federal system where centralized power is balanced with local initiative.

In the long run, we believe that the shape of future systems will depend not on technological agendas, but on the underlying shape of the organization. When the technology becomes truly great, it will become transparent, expressing not its own imperatives but those of the business. Current debate over whether the computer architecture of the future will be LAN-based or mainframe-based or even cooperative is in a sense foolish, for it deals with only the limited choices we have available now. Ultimately, computer systems will be like phone systems—so unobtrusive that they will just shape themselves around the organization's human lines of communication and command. Then people will return to debating what is really important—not computer architecture, but business architecture.

## Developers' Point of View

We hope that this book will find a wider audience than just developers, but undeniably we write from the developers' point of view. If your interest in cooperative processing is not academic, but aimed at getting something built, this book is for you.

We write from the trenches. What is in this book we learned by doing. John Tibbetts designed, and led the team that built, one of the first-wave SAA applications that debuted at IBM's May 1989 announcement. He and developers from the other inner-circle SAA vendors have met regularly to share experiences and trade suggestions. In a sense, this book represents the accumulated wisdom of this group. Put simply, this is what all of the developers say they wish they had known before embarking on their development projects.

We had no interest in rewriting the SAA manuals or in "bringing together in one place"—as many technical books like to claim—all of the disciplines required for building cooperative processing applications (anyway, our publisher was not interested in a nine-volume set). We assume that most development-minded readers understand basic system design, are familiar with database technology, know their COBOL, and might even have glanced at some SAA documentation. Our principle of inclusion has been: stick to information that is vital for cooperative processing development and that is available nowhere else.

This explains why the depth of our analysis is not uniform, but has shallow spots and deep spots like a lake ridged with sandbars. Where the material is familiar, we skim the surface and concentrate on evaluation rather than explanation. Where the material is new and hard to assimilate, we get specific, with algorithms, pseudocode, demos, and detailed diagrams.

## How to Read This Book

Unlike a reference book, where you can turn right to the areas that concern you, this book needs to be read from the beginning. Early chapters introduce terminology, concepts, and ways of framing the problem that persist throughout the book. We make a fairly iconoclastic case, and we would like to have you with us from the beginning.

The material gets increasingly technical as the book progresses. Executives, managers, marketing people, and interested observers, even those with no technical background, ought to find the first five or six chapters enlightening. We have tried to keep even the later sections accessible and jargon-free, so nontechnical readers may be able to stick around for quite a while.

Part I, "The Case for Cooperative Processing," puts the cooperative solution in its historical, sociological, and (dare we say?) metaphysical context. This section also introduces VIDOR, the sample cooperative processing application that crops up throughout the book as a running illustration for many concepts.

Part II, "Architecture for Cooperative Processing: SAA," is where most of the SAA-specific material is concentrated. Even people who feel well grounded in SAA structure and terminology might find some new angles here. Though the middle three chapters of this section are named for the three SAA common layers, they aren't the standard litany of interfaces and components. We focus instead on underlying issues, little-noted nuances, and practical implications for cooperative processing.

Part III, "Distributed Design Models," lays out a number of design principles for distributed—that is, multiplatform—systems. Its last chapter introduces some basic principles of object-orientation, a concept whose significance for cooperative processing can hardly be overstated.

Part IV, "Implementation Profiles," shows these design models embodied in concrete bundles of componentry. In these five chapters, we evaluate actual software components—some purchased, some purchased and modified, many built from scratch—that a development team will employ to put a system together. The last chapter sketches in the design models and implementation profiles that underlie a working cooperative processing system. By this point, we believe, a motivated team led by a talented designer will be ready to set off on its own.

## The Place of SAA

. . . *Using SAA* is our subtitle, but this is not an SAA book. We are not interested in exploring, explaining, or promoting SAA per se. Our look at the SAA interfaces, for example, is somewhat eccentric; those who want a solid introduction to SAA in all its glory would do better elsewhere. Cooperative processing is our concern, and these days we think that it is SAA's concern as well. Thus we devote a large section in the middle of the book to exploring what SAA has to offer, but always as the means to an end.

We believe that SAA is currently the system architecture (some use the term "enterprise architecture") with the most promise for the widest audience. Even better, SAA seems to be converging with other system architectures. Much of what we say here about SAA will end up being applicable far beyond the IBM world, if there will even be such a thing as a strictly "IBM world" in the future. IBM has shown unprecedented flexibility and a genuine eagerness for alliances with other vendors and with industry standards bodies. For IBM shops interested in moving toward open, multivendor solutions, SAA is definitely the place to begin.

## Terminology

As we wrote, time and time again we ran into the industry's fuzzy, situational use of terms like "architecture," "protocol," "client machine," "GUI," "front end," and "server." We have settled, sometimes arbitrarily, always painfully, on single meanings for terms like these. We have tried to be consistent without being academic or obscure.

## Acknowledgements

This book evolved from a class—"Cooperative Architecture and Design"—that has been widely presented by our company, Kinexis, over the past several years. We thank all who attended for their questions, objections, and affirmations.

Our clients have kept us in business and also in touch with "real-world" concerns. Thanks especially to friends at Tesseract Corporation, Metropolitan Life Insurance Company, Continuum Corporation, and Digitalk.

Colleagues at SHARE, GUIDE, OOPSLA, and other organizations have offered consistently stimulating feedback.

IBM has provided resources, information, and encouragement. We have been especially inspired and challenged by our associations with Diane Baron, Murray Berk, Cliff Reeves, and Earl Wheeler. We join many others in our regard for the late Bob Berland, probably the most effective person at IBM in articulating SAA's real meaning to the industry.

Thanks to all members of the informal but intense Tier A vendor's "club," whose hard-won wisdom shows up on nearly every page of this book. Jerry Grochow has been an especially helpful colleague.

We salute Gary Durbin, Cheryl Paterson, Joyce Pilgrim, and the rest of the Intuition team at Tesseract Corporation.

We also thank the late Chuck Balsly, publisher of *SAA Age*, who got us started on our writing career, and John Desmond of *Software Magazine* who has helped it along.

Special thanks to Eben Sprinsock, who not only gave us invaluable help in getting this book in shape, but who also has, over our long association, proved that the concepts we present here really can be made to work.

We want to thank also: Ken Gardner, Barbara Levin, Tom New, Judy Tupes, Dick Derringer, Bill Gladstone, Diane Cerra, Geoffrey Staples, Steve Manes, Stuart Bernstein, and—for their forbearance—our families and especially our children, Hal and Emily Tibbetts and Rachel Flynn.

## Trademarks

and SAA are registered trademarks of International Business Machines, Inc.

Choreographer is a registered trademark of Virtual Machine Corporation.

CommonView and C++/CommonView are registered trademarks of Glockenspiel Limited.

Crosstalk is a registered trademark of Digital Communications Associates.

DEC and DECforms are registered trademarks of Digital Equipment Corp.

Dustbuster is a registered trademark of Black and Decker.

Easel is a registered trademark of Easel Corporation.

IEE is a registered trademark of Hayes Microcomputer Products, Inc.

OSI is a registered trademark of On-Line Software, Inc.

Post-It is a registered trademark of Minnesota Mining and Manufacturing Company.

Power Nozzle is a registered trademark of Consolidated Foods Corp.

SNA is a registered trademark of Micro-Integration, Inc.

SQL and SQL-Forms are registered trademarks of Oracle Corporation.

Toolbook is a registered trademark of Asymmetrix Corporation.

UNIX is a registered trademark of Bell Laboratories.VM is a registered trademark of MVS Software, Inc.

XTree is a registered trademark of Executive Systems, Inc.

X.25 is a registered trademark of Dynatech Packet Technology, Inc.

InFront is a registered trademark of MultiSoft, Inc.

ISDN is a registered trademark of Mitel Corporation.

King's Quest is a registered trademark of Sierra On-Line, Inc.

Laura Ashley is a registered trademark of Laura Ashley Limited.

Level5 Object is a registered trademark of Information Builders, Inc.

Lotus and 1-2-3 are registered trademarks of Lotus Development Corporation.

Microsoft Windows and MS-DOS are registered trademarks of Microsoft Corporation.

Mozart is a registered trademark of Mozart Systems Corporation.

MVS is a registered trademark of Landmark Systems, Inc.

OSF, Motif, and OSFMotif are registered trademarks of Open Software Foundation, Inc.

# Part I

# The Case for Cooperative Processing

At this early stage in their history, cooperative processing applications are hard to build. Most observers believe that the effort is worthwhile, but it still falls to those of us who promote this computing style to make the case.

Cooperative processing offers great potential for more efficient, more powerful, more integrated, more effective large-scale information systems. These new systems, in turn, can give businesses a badly needed boost as they head toward the twenty-first century. Cooperative processing systems can vastly improve an organization's ability to serve customers, expand into new markets, and essentially redefine the scope and structure of its business.

Cooperative processing has emerged at a time when LAN partisans predict the disappearance of the mainframe as we know it and when corporate I/S departments respond with either increased isolation or complete capitulation. We advocate cooperative processing, not as a middle ground between these two powerful communities, but as a way for each to achieve its full potential, working together in systems more vast and powerful than anything we have seen so far.

# 1

# *The Two Worlds*

This book is about getting computers of different design and ancestry to work together. This sounds commendable and even fairly elementary, but it has turned out to demand major feats of diplomacy.

One of the difficulties, as this chapter shows, is that large enterprise mainframes and small desktop PCs do not have much natural affinity. They are both computers, of course, but then whales and rabbits are both mammals; this doesn't mean they can easily interbreed. To treat mainframes and PCs as just different models of the same thing is a serious mistake. From chip to screen; from ergonomics to aesthetics; historically, technologically, and culturally, they represent two worlds. There are fundamental differences in what these two kinds of computers do, how they do it, and on whose behalf. Bringing them together at this late date promises remarkable synergy, but the obstacles are great.

## The Mainframe Legacy

If you have worked in computing for more than 10 years, the first computer you encountered was bigger than you were (if you were a graduate student at the time, the computer was probably bigger than your *apartment*). It was hugely expensive, hugely complex, and so heavy that it needed specially built housing. It almost certainly belonged to a corporation or university, and it was surrounded by all sorts of bureaucratic policy and protocol, like most assets in the multimillion-dollar range. The computer was kept isolated from the rest of the organization in an air-conditioned "glass house," and only highly trained specialists could get it to do anything.

Even as mainframes shrink in size, they remain figuratively bigger than a person. Mainframes (and midranges and minis) are machines for communities. Their cost, power, and capacity make them suited to handle the complex, concurrent needs of large organizations. Corporate culture has shaped not only the policies that surround their use, but *their very design.*

3

Sitting as they do at the center of organizations, mainframes have acquired awesome responsibilities. These machines store and maintain extremely valuable resources, from engineering diagrams to crucial corporate data. They also hold a less-recognized but equally valuable resource: rules, formulas, and procedures that may represent years of development work—what we call "function." It is a tenet of the mainframe world that this data and function must be safeguarded from falling into the wrong hands, being corrupted, or being imprudently altered. Enormous effort goes into figuring out how to make information accessible to the people in the organization who need it and inaccessible to the people who don't. In a system with thousands of users at multiple locations, this is a major concern.

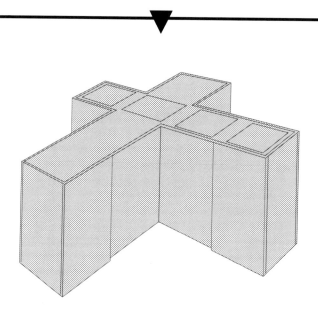

## TO THE MAINFRAME WORLD, A COMPUTER IS:

- A big, expensive, corporately owned machine.
- Used as a repository of data and function.
- Kept under centralized control.
- Carefully managed, especially with an eye to keeping resources secure.
- Used only by people with special training.

Getting a system this complex to work has become a specialty all its own. This is another characteristic of the mainframe world. Most any organization with a mainframe computer has a separate information systems department that programs and maintains the system. I/S people stand between the computer and the people in the organization who actually want the orders processed, the profits projected, the mailing lists updated, and the personnel files maintained. "The priesthood of the glass house," these I/S professionals have been called, interpreting the arcane mysteries of the computer for the rest of the company.

Outside of the glass house, out in the departments, mainframes are unaccommodating to the people they serve. Users sitting in front of "dumb terminals" feel pretty dumb themselves. They face an ugly screen, a complete lack of flexibility, and a time frame based on computer capacity rather than user need. I/S people often exercise great ingenuity in programming mainframes, but, once that job is done, humans interact with mainframes in a highly routinized, mechanized way. Mainframes do many things efficiently, but exploiting the intelligence of their users is not one of them. It often seems like the machine is using the people, not the people using the machine.

## The PC World

Many high-tech business people have never encountered this type of monster processor. To them, a computer is a small, self-contained desktop machine—affordable, forgiving, and empowering.

In nearly every way that the mainframe imposes itself on the user, the PC adapts instead. Where mainframes treat the user as an inconvenient and low-quality input device, PCs make user convenience paramount. They feature dazzling user interfaces, using color, graphics, sound, video, and keyboard alternatives to make programs easier to learn and use. Software written for PCs is organized around human-style tasks and mimics the way that people actually like to work. The interactive PC user interface style encourages creativity and gives instant feedback.

PCs emphasize access. No climate-controlled high-security glass house here. PCs invite users to insert disks, unscrew the back and fool around with the innards, install boards, attach auxiliary devices, add monitors, switch keyboards, and so on. Since, in most situations, nothing done on a PC can hurt anyone else, users have a great deal of freedom to experiment.

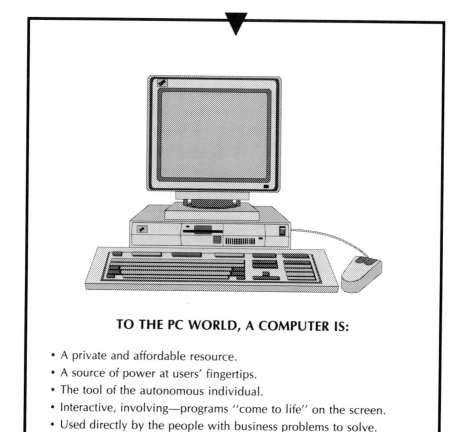

## TO THE PC WORLD, A COMPUTER IS:

- A private and affordable resource.
- A source of power at users' fingertips.
- The tool of the autonomous individual.
- Interactive, involving—programs "come to life" on the screen.
- Used directly by the people with business problems to solve.

Clearly, a PC is not just a miniature mainframe; it is a wholly different kind of machine. A mainframe is like a train; a PC is like a car. A mainframe is a 35mm movie in a theater; a PC is a videocassette. Mainframes lie within the venerable technological tradition of doing large jobs for large groups; PCs represent a newer style of putting less powerful but more responsive technology in the hands of individuals.

For a long time, the very attributes that make PCs so attractive to end users limited their usefulness in a corporate setting. An autonomous individual, however productive, has limited value to a large organization until he can start interacting with more centralized resources.

## Changing the Balance: PCs into LANs

PCs scored their initial success with personal-level jobs that mainframes had either ignored or done poorly, such as word processing, graphics, and spreadsheets. When PCs took up the slack, it was a great liberation. Anyone who has waited minutes to get a simple calculation done on the mainframe or waited years to get a new application from the always-backed-up I/S department remembers the giddy feeling of freedom and power that came with having her own machine.

Seated at their PCs, users suddenly found that the dark art of "programming" wasn't really so mysterious. Desktop hardware and the tools designed for it made it possible for everybody to be a programmer. Once a user had written a successful spreadsheet for tracking her own customer orders, why not write one that her colleagues could use too? And then a bigger one for the whole department? The whole division?

To take on these more ambitious tasks, PC users started hooking their machines together into networks, usually local area networks (LANs), that were able to handle larger and more complex jobs than any single machine could (Figure 1-1). And they began casting an eye toward more and more enterprise-level duties and resources.

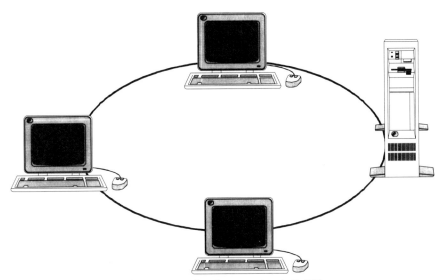

**Figure 1-1.** *Local area network (LAN)*

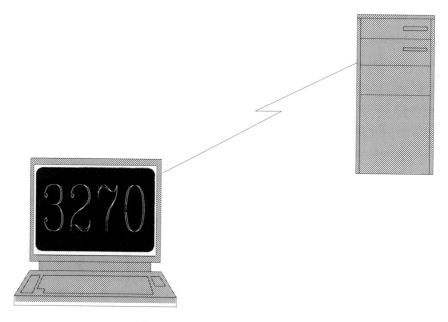

**Figure 1-2.** *Terminal emulation*

## Attempts at Linkage

Almost from the first appearance of PCs in an office, people have tried hooking them together with mainframes. The synergy between the two technologies is obvious. Mainframes are strong on data and function but weak on human factors; PCs empower human users but, even in a LAN configuration, have limited capacity, power, and manageability. For over a decade now, different techniques for linking the two sorts of machines together have been tried.

### *Terminal Emulation*

Terminal emulation—the earliest, the easiest, and still the most widespread form of linkage—gets the PC to mimic a dumb terminal (Figure 1-2). It evolved as a space-saving measure. Many people found themselves with both a terminal and a PC on their desks: Two keyboards, two monitors, and lots of redundancy. Enterprising companies soon developed hardware and software that lets a PC switch into a mode where it simply emulates a terminal. (This is the same impulse that has led to fax machines that do double duty as copiers.)

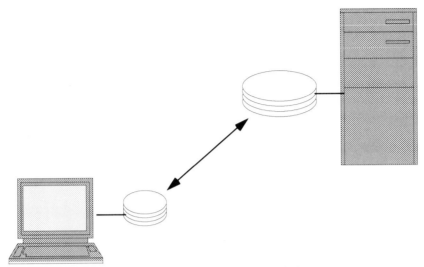

**Figure 1-3.** *Micro-mainframe link*

Terminal emulators work by shutting off about 98% of a PC's capabilities and using it only as a window into the mainframe. This is something like using your car as a sofa. In terminal mode, a PC looks and behaves like a 3270. All of its local intelligence is temporarily lobotomized. Still, terminal emulation gives a person who uses his PC for local applications a way of getting in touch with the mainframe when the need arises without having to turn to an entirely separate machine.

### Micro-Mainframe Links

Micro-mainframe links (Figure 1-3) represents an important next step in linkage. This technology grew directly out of the frustrations that came with having a schizophrenic terminal-emulation machine on the desktop. In terminal mode, an emulation machine would display a set of numbers needed for a PC application, but the user would have to write these number down on a piece of paper, switch computer modes, and reenter the numbers into the spreadsheet. Micro-mainframe links let a PC application pick up and directly integrate data downloaded from the mainframe.

It's not just a question of convenience; it's an issue of integrity. There's a true story about an international petroleum company that made a disastrous business decision based on wildly incorrect information. The company had a well-controlled I/S organization with decades of auditing and checking procedures in place. The projections in question had been extensively calculated and controlled at every level. But when a secretary copied the figures from the 3270 screen to enter them into a spreadsheet program on her PC, she transposed two figures, fed them into the spreadsheet wrong, and presented to the board of directors a printout that appeared to have all the authority of I/S behind it but was in fact no more reliable than a set of handwritten calculations. This is the sort of eminently human error that computers, if they can do anything, ought to be able to prevent.

Thus, micro-mainframe products build an extension cord between serially running applications so that files can be passed from the mainframe to the local application. The technology does not usually permit information to go the other way, however; input from the PC application cannot make any changes in the mainframe database. (I/S departments were already nervous about letting PC applications get hold of the enterprise's central store of data; the possibility of their being able to update it was appalling.) A micro-mainframe linkage clearly preserves the notion of two applications running. For example, the user may see a split screen with mainframe data on one side and PC files on the other.

## Cooperative Processing

Cooperative processing (Figure 1-4) takes a quantum leap ahead. This technology does away with the notion of two separate applications and calls for a single application that spans multiple platforms. We are no longer talking about an application that lives on one machine and occasionally reaches out to the other to fetch or report some information. A cooperative processing application truly spans the two. This requires not only significant redesign on one or both sides, but some fundamental reconceptualization as well.

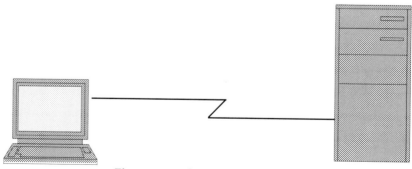

**Figure 1-4.** *Cooperative processing*

# 2

# *Why Cooperative Processing?*

Cooperative processing has been envisioned for a long time but has only recently come within reach. Advances in technology now make it possible for an application to alternate between glass-house and desktop platforms as the task at hand dictates. The result is a "virtual computer" that is both centralized and dispersed, both rugged and responsive. It's like some mythological creature with the strength of a lion and the beauty of a butterfly.

Cooperative processing systems are hard to build, but they solve many problems. In a good cooperative processing system, both mainframe and PCs have their strengths leveraged and their power enhanced. Chores that one platform found burdensome are taken over by a machine better suited to handle them. The organization benefits most of all. It gets systems that are more productive, more efficient, and often revolutionary (as we shall see later in this chapter) in the way they can bring a company's customers and its products closer together.

## Cooperative Processing Defined

The definition of cooperative processing is a controversial (and unfortunately highly politicized) topic, so we want to clarify now what we mean by that term. The definition that follows seems to us the one that is most widely observed in the development community and the one that opens up options rather than closes them off.

Cooperative processing (Figure 2-1) is:

1. A distributed processing system that involves two or more machines, where
2. One of the processors is a "front-end machine" devoted to user interface, and
3. The user is presented with the image of a single application.

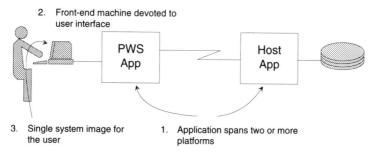

**Figure 2-1.** *Cooperative processing's three-part definition*

The first point identifies cooperative processing as a subset of **distributed processing**, which is one of the two primary branches of computing. "Distributed processing" refers to an application that involves two or more processors, as opposed to **local processing**, where an application runs entirely on a single machine.

The second point specifies that only those distributed processing systems that use intelligent, programmable front-end machines as full partners can qualify as cooperative processing systems.

The third point distinguishes cooperative processing from a simple micro-mainframe linkage. As far as the user is concerned, the only machine involved is the one she is sitting in front of. There is no split screen, no blinking cursor to indicate that the mainframe is being called, no change in the look of the screen as a different processor takes over. Entirely behind the scenes, a cooperative processing application switches as required from one platform to another, accessing the mainframe database for a lookup, recalculating figures on the local workstation, updating a remote database. The user neither knows nor cares where the lights are blinking.

---

### COOPERATIVE PROCESSING: A MARKETING TERM

Part of the difficulty over a definition for cooperative processing comes from the fact that it is a *marketing* term, not a technical one. It appears nowhere in the technical literature. It does not mean anything specific at the development level. It is like the term "sportscar"—not precise enough to be useful to an engineer or a mechanic, but highly evocative for salesman and consumer. Like "sportscar," "cooperative processing" bundles together a package of attributes under a descriptive name. It provides, for example, a great way to explain to a typical computer-illiterate CEO that he can get a PC-looking application backed up by a big machine full of enterprise-level data and function. To an implementer, however, "cooperative processing" is only a loose category that can encompass a wide range of designs, components, and linkages. In the more technical sections of this book, we often use the general term "distributed processing" instead of the more specific "cooperative processing."

---

The fundamental design guideline for cooperative processing systems is probably that *each machine does what it does best.* The real benefits of linking processors come when you take full advantage of each one's characteristics within a system where they can complement each other. Terminal emulation and micro-mainframe links fail to exploit the enormous power of the intelligent workstation; current "downsizing" philosophy underutilizes the mainframe just as badly.

Designers of cooperative systems have to take a fresh look at what each side really does do best. The key to application structure often lies with the less obvious abilities of each platform, as we will see in the next chapter, so it is important to get past conventional wisdom about PCs and mainframes.

## THE POWER NOZZLE STORY

For many years, John Tibbetts has explained the theory of cooperative processing by telling this story:

> Several years ago on a Saturday afternoon I was vacuuming the front room with my Hoover Power-Nozzle canister model S3271. A Power Nozzle is an attachment to the main vacuum-cleaner canister that is used especially for carpets. A small motor at the end of the Power Nozzle spins a brush that kicks up dust from the carpet; then the main canister can pick up the loose dust with much less suction than it would need otherwise. By dividing the vacuuming job into two distinct tasks, Power Nozzles do a very good job.
>
> As I was guiding my Power Nozzle around the rug, I realized that I had in my hands a mechanical cooperative processing system! Hoover had done exactly what we system architects talk about. By applying a small amount of energy at exactly the place in the system where the problem lay, Hoover had boosted efficiency enormously. Probably only 10% of the energy of the vacuum system goes to the motor at the tip of the Power Nozzle. But, because this energy is directed right at the dust embedded in the carpet, it doubles or triples the power of the system as a whole.

> Without power-nozzle technology, the only way to vacuum this well would be to increase the suction of the main canister two or three times. You would end up with a motor so powerful it would blow fuses and a canister so heavy that you couldn't drag it around the house.
>
> Many computing systems rely on what we might call "big-canister" architecture. Companies invest in ever larger and more powerful mainframes to get the power they need. These mainframes provide powerful central engines, but down at "floor level" they don't serve individual users very efficiently.
>
> Other systems take the opposite approach and use what I call "Dustbuster" architecture, in honor of those hand-held, cordless vacuum cleaners. Dustbusters are great for sucking up small localized messes, but you'd hate to clean a whole room with one. In the computer world, Dustbuster architecture scatters hundreds or thousands of PCs around an organization. These PCs work fine for activities relating to individual productivity, but they're a flop at working together to provide centralized community services.
>
> When a system needs to deliver both strong central computing and powerful end-user services, power-nozzle architecture is the way to go.

## What Cooperation Can Produce

Like so many technologies in history, cooperative processing seems to have emerged at just the right moment. The breakthroughs that make cooperative processing possible—in user interfaces, connectivity, and distributed databases, as well as in the emergence of standards that govern all of these—could not have come along at a better time. Businesses desperately need the new style of computing that these new technologies make possible.

Another way to look at it, of course, is that cooperative processing has been feasible in an abstract way for at least a decade. If the pieces have begun coming together over the past few years, it is because the effort now seems worthwhile. Old methods have run out of steam. Computing is ready to make the leap into new-style cross-platform applications that can extend their benefits to whole new classes of users and offer to these users a wider range of capabilities than has previously been possible.

## A Case Study: Movies on Video by Computer

The sample cooperative processing application that will turn up occasionally through the rest of this book—the imaginary but devoutly-to-be-wished VIDOR videocassette catalog and order system—grew out of a particularly dramatic business crisis.

Imagine a company called Hydra Film Classics, founded in 1951 by a Buster Keaton fan. Hydra toils away for years distributing 16mm prints to film societies, revival theaters, and college campuses. The company responds to the boom in interest in classic films in the 1970s by acquiring reproduction rights to more films, printing up a nice catalog, opening a number of branch offices, and—since a good Buster Keaton fan finds technology irresistible—buying its first computer.

At first, this small computer runs primarily order-entry and inventory-control systems. It is used by clerks who for years handled the same processes on paper. As orders come in by mail, telex, and phone, someone in the back office enters them, late in their life cycle, into the computer.

Over the years, as the company grows (Figure 2-2), the system's terminals move beyond the back room, on to more and more desktops, and outward into the field offices. Outlying sales reps learn to use the terminals to check product availability and get orders processed fast.

Then . . . crisis and opportunity! The videocassette revolution turns the classic film distribution business upside down. Hydra switches from 16mm films to videos and realizes that it has entered an almost entirely different field. Its relatively small group of regular institutional customers gets replaced by a vast public eager to watch good movies at home. There emerges a lucrative new market made up of the video stores that spring up on every corner, libraries, schools, clubs, restaurants, and especially individual collectors. The ordering and fulfillment process is less predictable, acceptable turnaround time shorter, competition greater, clients more diverse and demanding. To thrive in this new environment, Hydra looks for ways to increase both the *kinds of customers* it can provide services to and the *kinds of services* it can provide these customers.

Luckily, computer innovation has been keeping up with home entertainment innovation. Hydra mobilizes its computer system to provide the competitive edge. A new cooperative processing application called VIDOR (VIDeo Ordering and Reference) brings Hydra's customers into direct touch with Hydra's product line and makes it unprecedentedly convenient and fun for these customers to browse, choose, order, and pay.

The VIDOR system is highly cooperative. At the back end, host-based transactions support the company's order-processing and inventory functions. The host can handle real-time order entry from high numbers of workstations or LANs connected to it. It also provides up-to-the-moment inventory levels on tapes in stock, checks on the availability of tapes that need to be ordered from the supplier, and places such orders electronically.

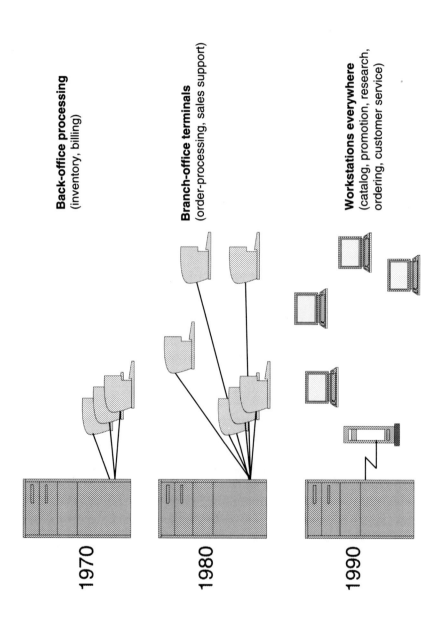

**Back-office processing**
(inventory, billing)

**Branch-office terminals**
(order-processing, sales support)

**Workstations everywhere**
(catalog, promotion, research, ordering, customer service)

1970

1980

1990

**Figure 2-2.** *Evolution of Hydra's information technology*

16

The front end provides a colorful, powerful, commodious interface to the user, whether Hydra employee or customer. Front-end systems are organized as local area networks connected via phone lines. VIDOR supports a movies database that functions as an electronic catalog and a very useful one at that, since it can generate lists of films selected by star, director, date of production, genre, and so on. It takes only a couple of seconds to find the names of all black and white films directed by George Cukor and starring Katharine Hepburn made between 1945 and 1955. VIDOR also contains an optional CD-ROM package of movie trailers, snippets of musical scores, and reproductions of advertising posters and selected stills. Of course, as cooperative processing requires, the user sees only a single system-image, whether he is dealing with local user-interface logic, LAN-level database, or inventory and ordering services that reside on a distant mainframe.

The system works successfully at every level, including the bottom line. A Hydra field rep with VIDOR on his desk is in a better position to advise and service the video outlets in his territory. A video store with VIDOR in house (for use by salespeople and possibly by customers at a kiosk) can become a real cinema resource center for customers. An individual purchaser with VIDOR on his home PC has a fabulous source of information, entertainment, and purchasing power.

## Reach and Range

Most companies wanting to stay competitive in the nineties face a similar challenge. Whether or not they confront an upheaval on the scale of Hydra's film-to-video revolution, their businesses are changing. Finding new ways to sell new products to new customers is imperative, and better information systems are the way to do it. Organizations need to rethink these systems, with an eye toward increasing what information consultant Peter Keen, in his book *Shaping the Future* (Harvard Business School, 1991), calls their "reach" and their "range."

"Reach" measures how far out from the central I/S function an organization's computing power is stretched. In Hydra's early days, its computer had very low reach: it was only used by back-office personnel working right where the computer was located. As the business matured and its use of information systems became more sophisticated, the reach was extended to the front office, then out to field offices, and out farther still to PCs in the stores, offices, and homes of its customers.

"Range" measures how interoperable a system is and how great a collection of services it encompasses. Range tends to increase as reach grows. At each step out from the center, the system encounters a wider variety of processes with which it has to interoperate. Its "job description" gets more and more inclusive. In the back office, the job is simply order-entry. When order-entry starts getting done out in field offices (for quicker order turnaround), it starts hooking up with the inventory and tracking functions and turns into a full sales-support system. And when the system reaches all the way out to the customer—video store, library media center, or individual film fan—it expands into a full-service sales tool capable of displaying, previewing, offering free samples, recommending, and seamlessly closing the sale. Thus, as reach extends farther out toward the ultimate end user, the range of integrated business services provided to those users increases too.

## Cooperation Makes It Happen

Industry after industry has started enlisting information systems to build sales, cut costs, open new markets, and extend business into profitable new areas. Banks move from human tellers to automatic teller machines (ATMs) and "home banking," (both of which, you may have noticed, serve as marketing tools for banks as well as financial tools for customers). Insurance companies empower agents, even independent agents, with cooperative applications that can access the enterprise database for instant projections, quotes, and underwriting information. Manufacturers link up electronically with suppliers to facilitate just-in-time inventory systems. Airlines transform agents from mere bookers into active salespeople by giving them the information and tools to put travel packages together and present them to customers. In every case, more comprehensive applications lead to better service, which leads to more business.

These new systems rely on cooperative processing, with its ability to link powerful, easy-to-use and fairly autonomous user PCs to large centralized stores of information, corporate policy, and computing power. They do not just expand the business but actually redefine it, redefining at the same time where computer systems fit into the overall scheme.

# 3

# *The Culture Clash*

Everybody seems to be in favor of cooperative processing. What's not to like? Management loves the idea of clever, powerful, easy-to-use, easy-to-sell applications with lots of reach and range. People in both computing worlds approve, in principle, of some sort of cooperation: I/S experts talk about needing better user interfaces; employees at their PCs are hungry for access to higher-level data. Customers flock to what few VIDOR-style products are available. With everyone in agreement, then, is it time to get started building these systems?

Not quite. Significant obstacles block the way, and the toughest ones are not technological but cultural.

## Unpeaceful Coexistence

In Chapter 1 we talked about computing's two worlds. Now we turn to The War of the Worlds.

Animosity between PC people and I/S people is a fact of life in any large organization today. Neither side seems to appreciate the other's strengths nor to understand the other's concerns. Each thinks that its technology alone can take computing into the future. Cooperative processing sounds great until you face the challenge of trying to unite into a single integrated system two groups of people who have spent most of the past 10 years avoiding each other.

Everywhere the same complaints arise. PC users out in the departments find the glass house bureaucratic, slow-moving, and indifferent to daily business needs like getting orders filled, product shipped, and reports produced. "Arrogance" is a word you hear a lot. PC users accuse I/S of clinging tightly to an outmoded monopoly on power and budget, and to some extent they are right. Like any centralized authority faced with a grass-roots uprising, I/S has been circling the wagons.

On the other hand, mainframe people regard PC users as irresponsible mavericks, ready to play fast and loose with years of accumulated knowledge and invaluable organizational resources. While there is territoriality at work here, they also have a good point. Integrity, security, documentation, backups, and corporate-level policy are concerns that PC people tend to dismiss. When I/S hears proposals to download more and more of the enterprise's resources to run on LANs, this seems as good an idea as parcelling out the gold in Fort Knox among several million citizens to keep in their homes. It may be more "democratic," but what happens to security, to centralized control, to uniform implementation of policy?

Such concerns border on the metaphysical. Here is one group steeped in responsibility for running large, complex systems where one error can cause losses in the millions and affect the jobs of thousands of people. The other group is interested in speed, responsiveness, flexibility, and optimizing the individual's performance. An organization can certainly profit from a healthy dose of both capabilities, but bringing them together will be a diplomatic coup.

▼

## CLASH OF CULTURES: A CASE HISTORY

We work with a large chemical company whose order volume is projected to increase tenfold by 1999. The company uses a mainframe transaction-processing system that was written 20 years ago in a hand-built teleprocessing monitor, which the employees don't know how to modify or maintain anymore. This system is out of capacity.

I/S is aware of the problem, and has put twenty of its best developers to work on it. This group is now in the second year of a 7-year study designed to come up with an enterprise data model *before* starting the design process for are placement system.

The grass-roots people at this company can't wait. They have orders to fill, so they have taken matters into their own hands. The man in charge of the company's international operations discovered Lotus 1-2-3 a few years ago and taught himself to build spreadsheets. He immediately stopped using the mainframe order system and set up a shadow network of his own. He now has three countries doing order-entry on Lotus 1-2-3 and using Crosstalk—bulletin-board software!—to communicate this information back to the United States. They are processing huge, high-value orders—tankloads of chemicals—on a system that has no notion of data integrity. I/S is horrified, certain that this guy is headed for a major disaster, which he well may be. On the other hand, he is getting his orders filled.

This head of international operations remains convinced that his company does not need mainframes, just lots of huge PCs that can run huge Lotus programs.

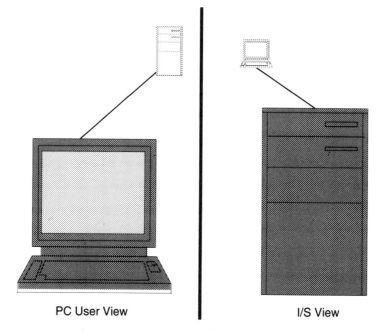

PC User View | I/S View

**Figure 3-1.** *Two views of cooperative processing*

## Each Side Wants to Dominate

The conflict sharpens up as soon as any cooperative processing discussion gets specific. Each of the sides tends to see cooperative processing from its own ethnocentric point of view. Like the much-imitated Saul Steinberg *New Yorker* cover with New York City in the foreground and the rest of the country stretching out vaguely in the distance, computer people see their own platform front and center and the other platform out somewhere near Nevada (Figure 3-1). Each side is convinced that in any sensible cooperative system they will "own" the application and have the other platform at their service as an accessory.

Mainframe people, with their tradition of centralized control, want cooperative processing systems in which PCs stick to spreadsheets and an occasional query but stay away from enterprise-level data. PC people believe that with sophisticated-enough LANs they can handle all the processing on the front end and keep the mainframe around as a "disk farm."

Neither view will get us very far. To build rich applications like VIDOR, a truly balanced system is needed. Such balanced systems are hard even to talk about within our traditionally bifurcated environ-

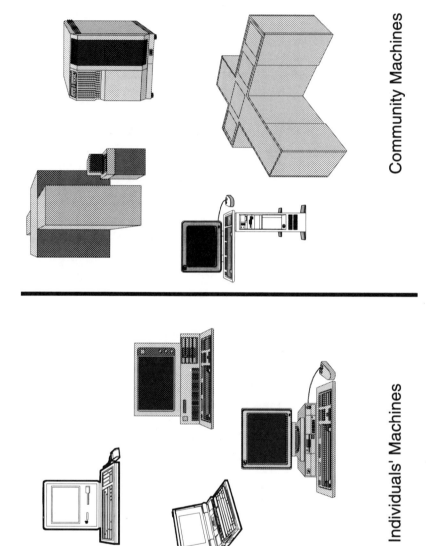

Community Machines

Individuals' Machines

**Figure 3-2.** *Roles, not hardware, are what counts*

ment, for nearly everyone is a partisan. There are few neutral thinkers; there is not even a neutral vocabulary.


## New Terminology

Vocabulary is a good place to start chipping away at old prejudices. The mainframe-PC distinction not only has lots of divisive history behind it; it also is obsolete for cooperative processing purposes. It locks you into a view of computing where model number is destiny. A designer will do better to look beyond the size, lineage, or innards of a machine and concentrate instead on the role it performs. The operative distinction here is not between mainframes and PCs but between **community machines** and **individuals' machines**, as shown in Figure 3-2.

A community machine is one that manages the resources of a group, whether an informal group of colleagues, a department, a division, or a whole multinational enterprise. Depending on the group's size, this machine could be a mainframe or a midrange. A PC that is being used as a LAN server is a community machine as well. If a machine's concerns and responsibilities transcend a single user's performance of his specific job, and if its constituency is larger than an individual, it is on the community side of the line.

As a family name for any machine performing a community function, we propose the old but nicely neutral term "host."

On the other side are machines that represent and amplify the effort of an individual. In a corporate environment, these are almost invariably PC-type machines; the larger machines that engineers call "workstations" are individuals' machines too.

We are going to use the term "workstation" in a general way to describe machines on the individual's side of the cooperative partnership. We want to emphasize here—as we will repeatedly—that the workstation should be thought of as the advocate of the individual user, not as a small piece of the community.


## Appropriate Jobs for Each

Since cooperative processing involves letting, as much as possible, each side do what it does best, it is important to make a fresh analysis of the sorts of jobs best done by hosts and those best done by workstations. Here it is important to go beyond the obvious. Nearly everyone would agree that the workstation should take care of the user interface and that the host should hold the large community database. The tug of war comes over all the function in between. This function is not monolithic;

looked at dispassionately, it can be divided up in ways that give each side a set of appropriate tasks but allow neither side to control.

## Community Machine: The Host

The host's role in a cooperative system is to manage community resources. By definition, this is the machine that concerns itself with allocating and safeguarding data and function belonging to a group. It enforces the community's policies. It represents the community's interests. Its horizons have to be as wide as the enterprise (department, division) as a whole.

### Database Services

The host is database-centered. It is the repository and the clearinghouse for the shared data of the organization. This database is a community asset, and the host has to keep it accurate and secure. The host is responsible for storing, maintaining, and updating this community data reliably and protecting it against system failures.

### Transaction Processing

People think of a community machine as primarily a database server, but function is a community asset as well. For example, the credit limit of a customer is clearly an enterprise-level asset, and so is the credit-check procedure that validates customer credit limits. Since rules are enterprise-wide resources, they should be held and enforced by the community machine. Enterprises exercise these rules in the form of orderly units called *transactions*, which ensure that complex community processing can take place without users colliding or function being incompletely applied.

### Device Services

User communities often find it convenient and sometimes essential to share printers, large file systems, multimedia equipment, and centralized time services. The community machine provides these unglamorous but vital services.

### Systems Management

Systems management—one of the under-recognized chores in commercial computing—includes such tasks as capacity planning, performance monitoring, network diagnosis, configuration management, software distribution, archiving, and resource accounting. These tasks are appropriate to a community machine with a wide view of the network underneath it.

## Individual's Machine: The Workstation

While the host takes care of the community, the workstation takes care of the individual user. This is a marvelous technology precisely because it enables a user to be a free agent in the way he does his job. Here we offer a radical but utilitarian assertion: A workstation's horizons should be as broad as its user's wishes, but no broader. Whatever an individual wants to do—competent or incompetent, productive or unproductive from the enterprise's point of view—the workstation helps him do it.

We do not imply by this that PC users are disloyal or unconcerned with the goals of the organization. In fact, individuals can make their best contribution to the organization when they are relieved of responsibility for complex, constricting enterprise-level concerns. One of the special geniuses of cooperative processing is that it lets the user concentrate on being an order processor, a profits projector, a shipping router, or a product developer rather than spending half of his time (and half of his machine's resources) as an outpost of the glass house, the executive committee, and the legal department.

### User Interface

The workstation provides the user, first and foremost, with a standard and powerful user interface. Graphical user interfaces are a unique capability of small, fast desktop machines, and they are far more than a cosmetic nicety. They make applications quicker to learn and easier to use and invest them with so much power that the whole user interaction is transformed.

---

### THE POWER OF USER INTERFACES

To appreciate the impact of improved user interfaces, look at the evolution of computer games since powerful PCs came on the scene. Fifteen years ago when we played the famous Star Trek game on the time-sharing machines at work, every move was a mathematical challenge. The teletype terminal would print out a little grid with Ks for the Klingons and Es for the Enterprise, along with a paragraph or two of status information and a command line for you to type into. You'd issue commands to scan or fire, type in numbers representing angles and headings, and slowly see a new grid reflecting the results. On a lightly loaded machine, the game iterated about every 30 seconds. It took an experienced computer person about a week to master the game.

Today an 8-year-old can play a much more complicated version of this game—with warp space and fourth dimensions and more kinds of weapons—that iterates at thirty times per second. He doesn't have to read, calculate, or type in anything—just track, aim, and fire. And it takes only about 15 minutes to pick up the moves. That's a 900-fold boost in productivity *just by changing the user interface.*

Virtually the same thing happens when users can click on "folders" and "garbage cans" instead of having to type instructions like "Delete * from emplist where empno = 1001." Soon workstation-based user interfaces will be so intuitively designed that users can fly databases and spreadsheets as effortlessly as kids fly video spaceships.

## Local Processing

Workstations have other talents to contribute to a cooperative processing system. Certain types of local processing lie in the natural habitat of the workstation. For example, if a user makes a typographical error, she shouldn't have to wait until that value has been sent 2,000 miles away to a mainframe to learn that February 30 is an invalid date. The workstation can also store locally useful data like county tax rates. Much of the functionality that used to be hoarded in the glass house can be relocated to workstation level—tasks like calculating an amortization schedule or prequalifying an insurance applicant. Keeping this kind of processing down close to the user greatly increases a system's performance.

## Data Integration

Workstations also provide powerful data integration services. A workstation can serve as a command central for all of the computing resources available to the user. In various windows on the screen, she can view a variety of programs—all so integrated that she can pull a paragraph from an e-mail that comes down and paste it into the document she's editing and then turn to the spreadsheet and pick up a set of figures. In an important sense, *the user becomes the application,* invoking the objects of the system at will. This contrasts with the culture we have grown up in, where the application on the mainframe periodically invokes the user.

## Summary

Notice that the community and individual sides both have an appropriate set of functions. The balance may vary from application to application and from business to business, but each is always a full partner with crucial jobs to perform. In a cooperative processing system, remember, there are multiple *processors,* each of which is fully capable of sophisticated computing. It follows that neither side can "own" the application; the benefits of cooperative processing come from synergy between the two.

# 4

# *The Negotiated Settlement*

Here, once again, are the significant strengths of our two newly defined cooperative platforms:

---

### HOST (COMMUNITY'S REPRESENTATIVE)

- Database services.
- Transaction processing.
- Device services.
- Systems management.

### WORKSTATION (INDIVIDUAL'S REPRESENTATIVE)

- Graphical user interface.
- Local processing.
- Data integration.

---

Notice that, while the two platforms have complementary strengths, they are also deeply adversarial. There is a natural tension between how the host works and how the workstation works. If we set each platform loose to pursue its agenda to the fullest, the two would collide with a crash. The last chapter's mainframe-PC standoff had more than ill will behind it.

The truth that we have to live with is this: *the goals of individuals and the goals of communities are often in conflict.* Finding a constructive balance between the two has been the work of social theorists and political philosophers for centuries, and now it is the work of systems architects as well.

The host, in its role as community advocate, is required to control access to its database and transactions in order to keep them secure and reliable. Yet everything about the workstation—its powerful user interfaces, integration services, and even the way it is screwed together—implies access. Satisfying the one often means undermining the other.

In our hypothetical VIDOR system, the front end is designed to make it almost effortless for customers to place orders. This serves customers well, but does it necessarily serve the company? Is effortless ordering a good corporate policy, if effortless ordering leaves the company open to fraud and foul-ups or to the possibility of double-filling orders that were inadvertently placed twice, or overextending credit, or sending adult videos to children? Look at the trouble that banks had before they got their ATMs programmed correctly, when customers could go around town withdrawing $200 from teller after teller, far exceeding the amount actually in their accounts.

As the reach of applications extends beyond employees to customers, increased user access has to be balanced with even more rigorous centralized control.

## Reconciliation through System Design

The fact that the front end and the back end have different agendas is what makes cooperative processing systems so rich and what makes designing these systems so tricky.

A designer will come to grief if she expects that the host, with its community responsibilities, and the workstation, with its user-at-the-center interfaces, will spontaneously fall into a comfortable division of turf. It is vital to recognize the conflict of agendas and to design in an accommodation between them. This accommodation belongs at the system-design level because mediation has to occur above the fray, so to speak. Neither of the interested parties can be expected to internalize the need to strike a balance. Each should be free to pursue its own agenda wholeheartedly, confident that the proper "mix" will be taken care of elsewhere. This is a notion of separation of powers that has worked well in government, families, and business partnerships. If a creative guy and a business guy start a small company, the creative partner should not spend much time worrying about balancing the books, and the business partner should not have to keep up on new shades of acrylic paint. Each is aware that the other's function is crucial and counts on it being done, but is not responsible for it.

### Workstation Proposes, Host Disposes

We propose a system design that not only retains but formalizes two separate spheres of influence—one devoted to workstation-based access and the other to host-based control as shown in Figure 4-1.

In the access region, at the front end of the system, the workstation reigns supreme. The user is free to do his particular job in any way that suits him—with hand-built applications, shrink-wrapped software, glass-house-created programs, or a combination of these. Whenever he wants to do something that involves accessing or updating community resources, this wish gets converted into a request to the host, which may or may not oblige.

The back end, the control region, checks all incoming requests according to its own policies and procedures *without assuming anything about the quality of the information it is getting from the front end.* It protects its treasure, so to speak, with a rigorous series of edits, audits, and security checks applied as a matter of policy to every incoming message without exception.

The front end, then, can only suggest changes to the enterprise resources; it cannot effect them. Only the back end can do this, and only after evaluating the suggestion according to all of the procedures that the enterprise puts into place. In other words, the user *proposes*, the host *disposes*.

### The Trust Line

We call the border between the two regions the "Trust Line" (Figure 4-2). All machines and applications in front of the Trust Line are

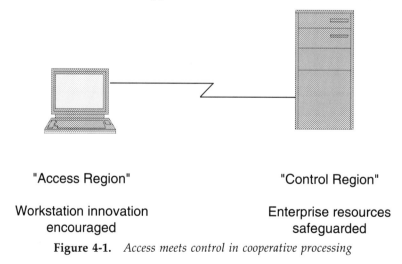

"Access Region"                                "Control Region"

Workstation innovation                     Enterprise resources
encouraged                                        safeguarded

**Figure 4-1.** *Access meets control in cooperative processing*

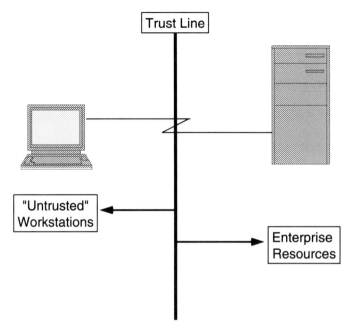

**Figure 4-2.**   *The Trust Line*

considered "untrusted" from the enterprise's point of view. This means that they cannot be entrusted with the ownership or maintenance of community resources. These resources live over on the secure side of the Trust Line, and proposals to alter them in any way have to clear an inside-the-trust-zone series of checks before the alterations can take effect.

If it sounds like a slander to call workstations untrusted, consider that their untrusted status is in fact their best guarantee of freedom. Just as someone can speak more freely when she is not the official spokesperson for an organization, a machine can work unconstrained when it is not held responsible for the paralyzing complex of enterprise-level concerns. Since the untrusted side has no resource ownership, it is allowed to be creative, wide-ranging, wide-open, and, in the best sense of the word, irresponsible. People not even employed by the company or interested in its policies—customers for example—can be allowed access to the untrusted zone. Your place of business can be open to the public if you don't keep your cash box there.

The trusted side, on the other hand, has little or no latitude for individual initiative. It is controlled, secure, centralized, and—under this setup—protected from even the most aggressive workstation input. The room in your business where you keep the cash box has to be locked up to keep the public out.

## Replicas Downloaded

If no enterprise resources are kept on the untrusted side of the line, does the workstation have to cross not only the border but long communication links to interact with the enterprise? No. A *replica* of any useful procedure or data can be downloaded to the LAN or even the individual workstation where it can be accessed efficiently and cheaply (Figure 4-3). The only constraint is this: as soon as it passes into the untrusted zone, it too becomes untrusted, even if it is completely I/S-created. The untrusted side never gets the only copy of any data or function; the definitive version stays safe behind the Trust Line. Whatever function runs on the untrusted side is always provisional and unofficial; no changes are made to the official data on the trusted side until this function is rerun behind the Trust Line.

For example, a Hydra sales rep might be able to give better service if she had a copy of the company's credit-check procedure on her workstation. She could verify a client's credit and approve his order immediately. However, before the actual order took effect at the enterprise level—the supply of tapes debited, the shipping department notified, and the client's account charged—the credit check would be run again on the other side of the Trust Line. This would guard against several

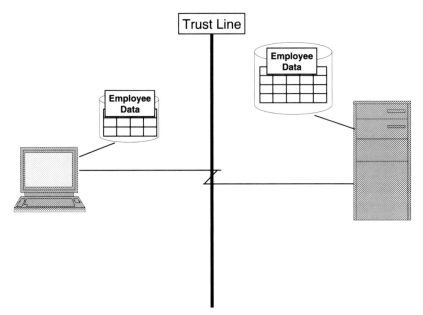

**Figure 4-3.**   *Replicas downloaded*

possibilities: the sales rep might have used the credit-check program incorrectly; the customer may have placed multiple simultaneous orders through different reps, driving his total order above the credit limit; the rep might be using an outdated version of the credit-check program; the rep might be conspiring with the customer to defraud the organization; somebody might have stuck a screwdriver in the rep's workstation, causing it to work crazy; the rep might be using a credit-check program she built herself that doesn't take into account a number of obscure rules unique to the company.

If the system extends its reach out to let the customer place orders directly, even worse mistakes or mischief could result from relying on him to verify his own credit on his own machine. The organization simply cannot afford to let an order go through on just the say-so of an untrusted workstation.

Thus, the Trust Line accomplishes the goal of leaving workstation initiative unencumbered while keeping community resources uncompromised. The untrusted state gives users unprecedented power and freedom. They are free to request data, take orders, grant credit, and authorize shipments. They can originate programs; invent tools; try out new software; install new boards; and take full advantage of having intelligent, programmable machines on their desks. Community assets are protected because *everything is checked at the border*. The security and integrity fears that the glass house has raised as a reason for curtailing the activities of users at workstations have disappeared.

▼

## AN OBJECTION: WASTE OF RESOURCES?

The negotiated settlement keeps enterprise assets secure behind the Trust Line by having the host check every incoming message scrupulously, disregarding—not even knowing—whatever preliminary checks or audits may have been run down nearer the user.

The objection arises that running checks twice on either side of the Trust Line is redundant and expensive. Isn't cooperative processing supposed to *conserve* resources? Won't the productivity gains that result from downloading some function closer to the workstation be wiped out if all this function has to be repeated farther up the line?

It is true that running a credit check twice per transaction costs more than running it just once. This is not redundant, however, since the check has a different function outside the Trust Line than inside. At any rate, front-end MIPS are very cheap, so the credit check on the workstation is not costly. MIP-intensive back-end checks cannot be eliminated, despite what some "downsizers" claim, without leaving enterprise resources unacceptably exposed.

The expense is minor in the overall scheme of things. Some edits are duplicated, but editing makes up only a small fraction of most applications' computing logic. Savings in other areas more than compensate. Once the back end no longer has to concern itself with the user interface, for example, significant cost savings result from reduced message traffic and cheaper presentation logic.

Admittedly, the Trust Line represents a conservative approach to system design. It may seem particularly conservative to people from the LAN world, who have not usually worried about safeguarding huge enterprise resources. In situations where security and integrity are not so important, such a firm line of defenses may not be necessary, but no large corporate transaction processing system can afford to forego it.

## Border Issues

The border between the trusted and untrusted zones is the critical element in the design. It cannot be left vague or ad hoc. Exactly where one side's sphere of influence stops and the other's starts has to be firm, clear, and architected into the basic structure of the system.

Where this border falls and exactly what happens there are topics for negotiation between the two sides. This negotiation may take place inside the head of the system architect, provided he truly understands the interests of each side, but it might be better to have representatives of the glass house and the departments actually sit down together and hammer it out.

Where should the Trust Line fall? How much of the application logic really needs to be locked away behind the Trust Line, and how much can be left accessible in front? How are requests from the untrusted side conveyed to the trusted side? What class of requests from the workstation will the host absorb, and how should they be structured so that the host understands them? What set of responses can the workstation expect back? What is the message protocol for each side? These and other issues call for an uninhibited give-and-take over the negotiating table.

The negotiation will result in a whole treaty's-worth of agreements, which should be formalized and documented. They will be quite specific. For example: The workstation is allowed to propose extending a customer's credit limit and will have to accompany this request with bank reference, major credit card number, and name and address of employer. Any order over $100 requires a driver's license number. If the workstation submits a proposed order, it will get back from the host a six-digit order confirmation number. The workstation is permitted to make noncontrived data requests (in SQL, for example), but only under certain circumstances. . . .

All issues up for negotiation will eventually be framed in terms of the messages going back and forth across the border. These messages are how the front end and the back end communicate—how all those proposals are submitted and confirmed. So one of the most important results of the negotiation will be a standard format for messages that both sides can understand, plus an agreement on the sorts of messages that are permitted. In fact, the entire relationship of the components in the system ends up embodied in the set of messages, called a "protocol," that each can send and receive.

### MESSAGES

The notion of messages may not be familiar to those who are not communications programmers or converts to the new discipline of object-oriented programming. The rest of us have been writing programs that run in a single environment and have not had to think about sending messages among processes. But once an application gets divided among platforms or into modules of any sort, it is necessary to develop a standard way that the parts can communicate with one another.

A message is something like a letter addressed and written according to a highly standardized format. A message comes with an address, states its purpose, and contains sufficient information to see that purpose accomplished. Message-based systems are widely used in cooperative processing; in fact, the use of standard messages is one way that such systems can offer the flexibility they do.

## LAN Topology

How does the Trust Line, which looks good in diagrams, fare in the real world? Actual commercial systems, much more complex than our one workstation linked to one mainframe, have several levels of "community" (department, division, region, U.S. operations, etc.) and several levels of community machines. Extending the trusted/untrusted model to more complex systems means establishing multiple intermediate

Trust Lines at various levels. The principle is always the same—separate community concerns from individual concerns and architect a firm border between the two.

### Cascading Trust Lines

As an example, look at the next-highest level of complexity from our one-workstation/one-host setup: a very simple local area network of PCs with one PC used as a LAN server to provide the network's gateway to the enterprise. The principles we see in this configuration can be extended to any number of cascading levels.

In a workstation-LAN-host configuration, the Trust Line can fall anywhere. Placement is up to the system designer (and the delegates to his negotiating conference). It depends upon the nature of the business, the machines in use, and the legacy systems that have to be accommodated. Consider a few possibilities, and notice how the dynamics of the system change as the Trust Line gets moved to one end or the other.

- **Untrusted Workstation.** A typical case would place the Trust Line right in front of the LAN server (Figure 4-4). This provides a good combination of security and accessibility. Since the trust zone extends all the way down through the LAN server, community resources live in close proximity to the workstations that will be using them, but they are still locked up.

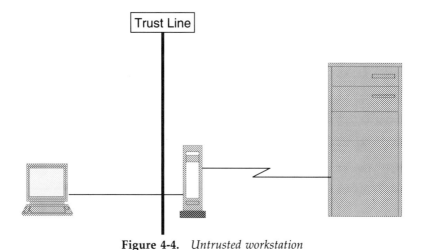

**Figure 4-4.** *Untrusted workstation*

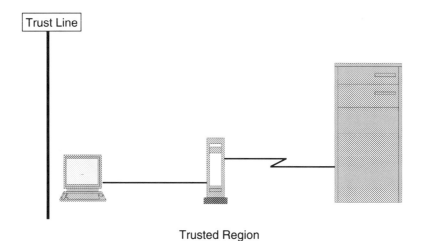

Trusted Region

**Figure 4-5.** *Trusted workstation*

- **Trusted Workstation.** Another possibility is to draw the line all the way down at the front end (Figure 4-5), essentially placing the entire system behind the Trust Line. A number of banks do this. They turn their teller workstations into trusted machines, depriving them of disk drives and literally locking the CPU in a cage. This is a perfectly good design point, and it is useful in certain highly con-trolled environments where it is possible to dictate the flow of work to workstation users. It essentially brings back the world of termi-nals. The biggest obstacle to this setup is user resistance. How many employees now using PCs would be willing to give up their disk drives and run only glass-house-supplied programs?

- **Untrusted LAN.** Alternatively, the Trust Line can go all the way over at the other end of the system (Figure 4-6), with everything except the enterprise host considered untrusted. An example of this is a federal agency we know of that has 2,000 LANs of doubtful security spread around the country. In this case, even the gateway machines are untrusted, so the Trust Line is all the way up inside the host machine. This setup sacrifices high-speed connections with local resources; it becomes necessary to go much farther over expensive communication lines to get to enterprise resources. Still, this is the best way to handle situations where the LAN cannot be counted on for security and integrity.

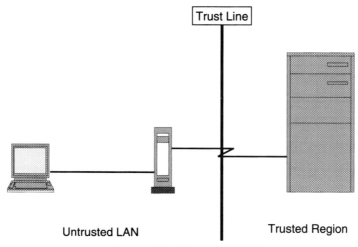

**Figure 4-6.** *Untrusted LAN*

The rule of thumb for positioning the Trust Line is this: *Enterprise responsibility starts behind the first locked door.* Any machine that someone can stick a screwdriver into should not be trusted, should never hold the definitive copy of any enterprise asset, and should not be authorized to make unilateral changes to enterprise resources. It is surprising how many organizations keep valuable resources on a physically vulnerable machine when they would never keep even a small amount of petty cash in an unlocked drawer.

### Heterogeneity and Homogeneity

When we look at real-world applications, the issue of heterogeneity within systems soon arises. Most organizations have to accommodate a great deal of diversity on the front end, and larger organizations might own several different kinds of host machines as well.

Under our Trust-Line architecture, heterogeneity on the front end is virtually unlimited (Figure 4-7). The credit goes to messaging. The front end and back end communicate through the Trust Line via messages so standardized that the back end has no idea whether a message has come from a PC, Macintosh, ATM, or burglar-alarm system. Thus almost any machine can participate at the front of a cooperative processing system. If the designer is willing to do the implementation work, there are no architectural constraints.

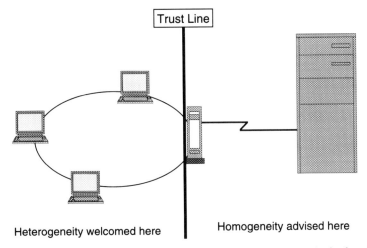

**Figure 4-7.** *Heterogeneity on the front end, homogeneity on the back end*

From the Trust Line back, on the other hand, architectural homogeneity is strongly advisable. A trusted environment has to provide security and integrity combined with good performance — easy enough when there is a single machine in the trust region, but difficult if there is more than one machine and *very* difficult if these multiple back-end machines are not homogeneous. The connections between trusted systems have to be unusually rich and multilayered to accommodate the variety of interactions: error-free communications, file connections, database connections, remote program access, transaction synchronization, etc. As of today, such robust connections are almost impossible unless the machines are architecturally compatible. Many people are counting on the emerging "open systems" movement to provide interconnections among heterogeneous platforms, but this is still well in the future.

If you need to get work done now, or 2 years from now, define your trusted platforms using homogeneous platforms. If you cannot avoid having to accommodate diverse host machines on the back end, you will have to consider each architectural platform trusted within itself but untrusted with respect to other architectures. Set up multiple autonomous trust areas that communicate with each other via the same procedure of messages and internal checks as any other untrusted-to-trusted communication.

## Summary

Many organizations find that the notion of the Trust Line clears up problems that have hobbled their system design for years. There seems to be no alternative way to envision end-to-end systems that encompass both individual initiative and enterprise security—certainly no alternative so simple and extensible.

In an ironic way, building the Trust Line is a good step toward uniting the two worlds. Good fences make good neighbors, as they say. Under the negotiated settlement, each acknowledges its limitations, gives up the illusion of autonomy, hands over certain functions to the other side, and starts seeing itself as a participant in a unified multi-platform system.

# Part II

---

# Architecture for Cooperative Processing: SAA

With the Trust Line showing a way around the sociological and political barriers to cooperative processing, we now move to the equally daunting practical problems. A cooperative processing system has to be built, operated, and maintained so that dissimilar pieces work together smoothly on a daily basis. Since separate groups of people will most likely be working on various parts of the system largely independent of one another, overarching standards and structures are critical.

To come up with a coherent set of standards that suits both sides, *designers* have to become *architects*. A system architect can fortunately get a great deal of the structure that she needs, predefined and ready to go, from one of the "system architectures" (sometimes called "enterprise architectures") that various vendors and industry-standards bodies have been devising over the last several years.

This section of the book looks in detail at the first and most widely implemented of the system architectures—IBM's Systems Application Architecture (SAA). As we will see, SAA was not designed primarily with cooperative processing in mind, yet its extensive framework of standard interfaces and protocols can serve cooperative processing systems admirably.

The aim in this section of the book is not to enumerate (yet again) SAA's components, but to explain and evaluate what SAA gives a cooperative processing-bound IBM shop to work with. Where SAA falters, or where it is simply insufficient for a given application, the architect must be ready to devise structures and interfaces of her own. Subsequent sections of the book tell how.

The following survey of SAA aims to point out to developers:

- What's there. SAA components and interfaces provide the infrastructure for a cooperative processing system.

- What's important for cooperative processing. The developer will not be using every piece and should know which are crucial and which can be discarded. Some parts of SAA are of dubious value to just about everybody; others may simply be irrelevant to a particular application.

- What's on the way. Many parts of SAA have been specified but not yet implemented. Since SAA is largely a framework for standards, the intention may be almost as good as the implementation. If a designer knows what interface is planned, she can come up with temporary work-arounds that will serve nicely until the real thing arrives.

- What's missing. In a complex system architecture, the holes are not always obvious. Often a development team discovers late in the design process that there is a void where they expected a crucial linkage, and then they have to do a lot of backtracking. In order to supplement the system architecture with a solid application architecture of her own, a designer should know ahead of time when the ball will bounce into her team's court.

Shops using a system architecture other than SAA can use this section as a model for their own analysis. As it turns out, the truly critical parts of SAA, those that get the most attention here, are those that SAA shares with most other system architectures. Even if you are not an SAA developer, do not be put off by chapters called "CPI," "CCS," and "CUA." Most of the fundamental issues, if not all of the specifics, are universal.

# 5

## *From Standards to Architecture*

Figure 5-1 sets forth the disheartening sight of the gulf between workstation and host platforms. Incompatibility looms everywhere. Languages, paradigms, and communication protocols are all mismatched to one degree or another. Yet cooperative processing depends on the two sides passing data and function back and forth in perfect concert. It's like putting a short fat guy and a tall thin guy in one of those vaudeville horse costumes and trying to get them to dance.

How can this gulf be bridged? Both sides are well entrenched. Bringing host applications and workstation applications into line by rewriting one or the other is out of the question. Common components and common structures, sufficient to let the two sides work together, have to be found.

Think of the two sides as two countries. In Chapter 4, they acknowledged their cultural differences, defined their spheres of influence, drew the borders, and set up border checkpoints. There remains the job of deciding how actual commerce between them will happen—what currency will they trade in, what language will they communicate in, whose laws will govern their interactions?

### Standards and Architecture

It is theoretically possible to define an ad hoc standard for every linkup in a cooperative processing system—perhaps 500 unrelated decisions. But who would want to do such a thing? For systems this complicated, it is much better to devise an integrated complex of standards—what is called in the industry an *architecture*. Designing a system without an architecture is as foolish as building a house without blueprints.

"Architecture" in the computer world has as many levels of meaning—technical and metaphoric, specific and general, precise and sloppy—as it does in the real world (when you read about "the

**43**

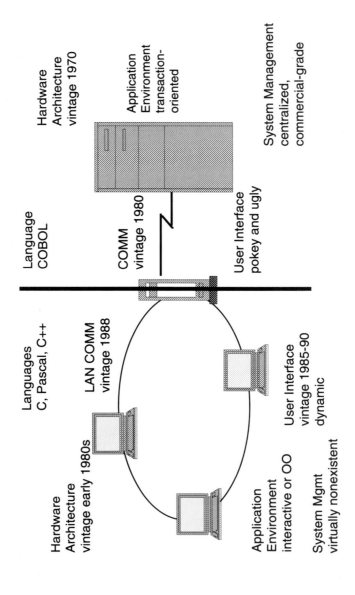

**Figure 5-1.** *The Grand Canyon of systems*

architecture of the English language," you know that the word has traveled far from the building trades). Here is a working definition: *Architecture is a formal set of standards that describes the relationship and interaction among various parts of a system or network of systems.*

For a sturdy cooperative processing system, the architecture must be complete enough to bridge all the technology gaps, establish all the relationships, and resolve all the issues—down to the specific componentry of a specific application. This is a vast job for any organization to take on, and fortunately none has to.

## System Architecture Plus Application Architecture

No building architect designs a structure totally from scratch. There are many standardized elements (ceiling grid systems, prebundled mechanicals, the proportions of a classical bay window) and many standard connections (how joists are secured to pillars, how columns are attached to a foundation, how exterior walls are connected to the structural frame). Similarly, a computer architect can pick up a great deal of the total architecture his system needs from a predefined set of standards called a **system architecture**.

System architectures have emerged in the last several years, largely from hardware vendors trying to bring consistency to their product lines. A few industrywide bodies, notably the Open Software Foundation (OSF), have also weighed in with architectures that they say will cross vendor lines and make software portable across whole segments of the industry.

None of these system architectures provides anything near a complete framework for cooperative processing systems. For one thing, all are fairly young and incomplete. For another, they are generic by nature. Every application will have unique requirements (relating to the job it has to do, the existing pieces it has to accommodate, etc.) that no off-the-shelf architecture can satisfy. A development team can plan on developing a great deal of its own application-specific architecture. These components and structures are the "custom cabinetry" of your system. Figure 5-2 shows that the total architecture required for cooperative processing will come partly from a system architecture and partly from an organization's own **application architecture**.

A strong application architecture is a very good investment. You should go beyond just patching up the holes in the system architecture you adopt. Time spent architecting your own application piece as well will pay off in a stronger design, and code that will prove more durable, flexible, and portable over the long haul. Most of the second half of this book deals with building application structures that cannot be

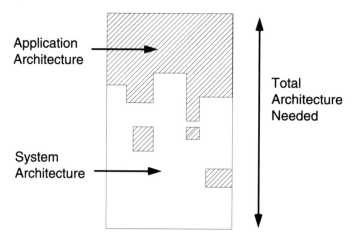

**Figure 5-2.** *System architecture must be supplemented with application architecture*

picked up from vendor-developed or industry-developed system architectures.

### Advantages of System Architectures

Whatever their shortcomings, system architectures offer so many advantages that it would be foolish not to adopt one.

First of all, a system architecture does a great deal of work for you. You may be able to find 70 or 80% of the component standards your system needs predefined so that you can snap them into place with little or no customization. They will set you up with significant chunks of architecture that you will have in common with other organizations.

Here is a second advantage of building your application upon a base of system architecture. Others in the industry—vendors, potential partners, merger/acquisition candidates—will be using the same standards, and if your company will be interacting with them you will want to be on the same wavelength. Our "two countries" can invent a private language for dealing with each other, but adopting English or French will keep them in better touch with the outside world.

### Architecture for Your Largest Machines

There are probably a dozen credible system architectures, some of which are listed below. Picking the right one is an important decision, but not as momentous as it may seem. Choosing an architecture—any architecture—is more important than which one you choose. Fortunately, the common components from several of the leading architectures seem to be merging; many interfaces of OSF and SAA, for example, are headed rapidly toward convergence.

▼

## SOME SYSTEM ARCHITECTURES

SAA (IBM)

NAS (Digital)

IIE (Unisys)

OSF, UI (Unix Coalitions)

CA'90 (Computer Associates)

Join up with the architecture most compatible with your biggest and most central machines. Such machines should determine your choice of system architecture because they are the most entrenched, intransigent, and hardest to reprogram.

## IBM Shops Need SAA

For any IBM shop, the choice is clear. IBM's Systems Application Architecture has been designed for IBM-legacy systems. It also represents IBM's direction for the future. If you have an investment in Blue mainframes, midrange machines, networks, IBM software, or even good relations with the IBM Corporation, adopt SAA for your strategic planning.

SAA has objective virtues, of course. It is the prototypical enterprise architecture. IBM essentially invented this category, and many of its ideas have been adopted by competitors. SAA has the resources of the world's largest computer company behind it, and IBM seems committed to supporting SAA over the long term. SAA offers probably the largest range of capabilities for commercial information systems. Finally, SAA seems to be on a convergence path with OSF, so it will position you to interoperate with the major players in any future market. But SAA is not *so* much better than any other architecture that it makes it worthwhile to jettison your installed base, change your affiliations, and go Blue simply in order to take advantage of it.

The next five chapters look at SAA in depth. Whether examining its history, evolution, contents, or underlying agendas, our aim is to see how we can shape this huge structure to our own ends, that is, implementing cooperative processing systems.

# 6

## *What Is SAA?*

SAA, and its icon (Figure 6-1), suffer from no lack of exposure, but many people remain unclear about its true nature and intentions. Is it hardware? Is it software? When is it going to get here? Or has it already come and gone?

IBM is partly at fault, for it has put out a number of confusing messages about SAA. At the same time, SAA has continued to change out from under any messages about itself, undergoing an almost incessant process of reorganization and refocus to keep up with changes within IBM and throughout the industry.

When SAA was first announced in March of 1987, IBM said this: "SAA is a collection of selected software interfaces, conventions and protocols that are being published." This remains the message that best sums up the true nature of SAA, despite later muddling.

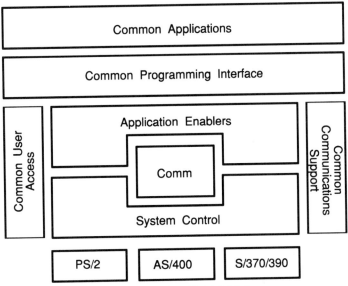

**Figure 6-1.** *The official SAA icon*

Notice that "interfaces, conventions, and protocols" are not things that you can go out and buy. (Apparently the IBM sales force has shown some lack of enthusiasm for SAA since, as one veteran sales rep put it, "What's there to sell except a bunch of manuals?") SAA has been hard for many people to get their minds around because it is so intangible. Essentially, it is just *a blueprint for how to put systems together*. It tells how things should be linked together, but it is neither the things to be linked nor the linkages themselves.

## SAA's Three Interfaces

The interfaces, conventions, and protocols referred to in IBM's statement are designed to give various hardware/software platforms a uniform look to the outside world. SAA has formulated this "outside world" in terms of three consumers of computer resources. This is perhaps SAA's major contribution to the art of systems architectures. We almost take this three-part distinction for granted now, but it was an innovative way of organizing hundreds of separate standards into workable categories. The three SAA consumers (Figure 6-2) are:

- Users.
- Programmers (either human or automated).
- Other computers.

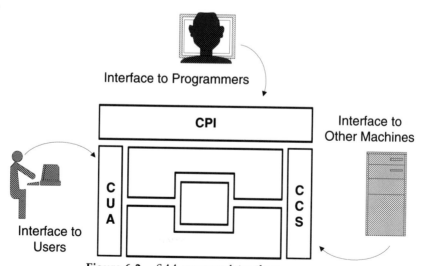

**Figure 6-2.**   *SAA accommodates three consumers*

To each of these, SAA offers a multifaceted interface:

- **Common User Access (CUA)** defines standardized rules of interaction between humans and the SAA platforms. These rules cover keyboard and mouse standards; conventions for data display; navigation through the application; and use of windows, icons, graphics, and so on. Note that CUA is a set of standards, not a bundle of code. The standards precisely define what the user of any SAA-inspired application should see, experience, and do.

- **Common Programming Interface (CPI)** implements standard languages in which programmers should write SAA applications and standard services that these programs can call upon. Services are fragments of commonly used code that handle basic tasks like accessing the database, displaying data or graphics to a presentation space, or talking to a communications line. The SAA CPI consists of programming interfaces, not code.

- **Common Communication Support (CCS)** is SAA's interface to other machines. It contains the protocols, or agreements, that let computers exchange a variety of data and messages over communications channels. The CCS contains protocols, not code.

- In addition to SAA's three "common layers," there is a top layer called **Common Applications (CA)**. We consider it largely a placeholder that shows where applications—those built by SAA-subscribing vendors and users plus those provided by IBM itself—fit into the structure.

## Is SAA a Product?

If our assertion that SAA is an intangible conflicts with what you have been led to believe, IBM is at least partly responsible. Their marketing message on SAA has often taken as its starting point "the four SAA platforms," as shown in Figure 6.3. This is a mistake of the tail-wagging-the-dog variety. It is true that IBM has committed to implement the SAA interfaces on four strategic platforms—OS/2, VM, MVS, and OS400. But saying that SAA *is* these four IBM platforms and, by extension, what they happen to have in common, gets it precisely backwards. (It also tries to sell customers precisely what they are not interested in; why make a long-term commitment to a product line?)

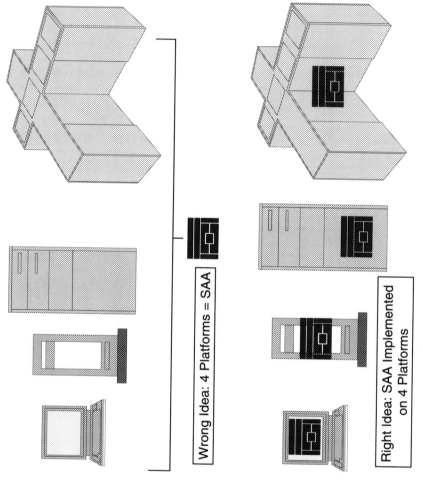

Wrong Idea: 4 Platforms = SAA

Right Idea: SAA Implemented on 4 Platforms

**Figure 6-3.** *SAA committed to four platforms*

52

It seems much more useful to emphasize instead that SAA is a blueprint for future directions that can be implemented on any platform, IBM or non-IBM. The IBM Corporation has decided to take four highly diverse operating systems and start them on the path toward interoperability (and eventually portability) using SAA as a gauge and a guideline. But SAA is being imposed on these platforms; it does not grow out of them. It is quite possible to build a fully compliant SAA system that contains no IBM hardware at all, just as you could achieve a totally "Laura Ashley" look without buying a single lampshade, pillowcase, or yard of wallpaper from a Laura Ashley store.

## Is SAA Proprietary?

Often you hear the objection that SAA is a "proprietary"architecture that will lock organizations into an exclusively IBM solution. To call SAA "proprietary" misses the point, for SAA is nothing but a framework for standards of many sorts—and a far-from-secret framework at that.

SAA selects, arranges, and interconnects publicly available components in a way that is visible to all. Every one of the components that SAA recommends is either "open" in the sense of being industry-controlled (SQL [Structured Query Language], COBOL, OSI [Open Systems Interconnect]), or else "published"—IBM-controlled, but available to all who want to read the manuals. None of the interfaces is "closed," that is, kept private, as many Apple standards have been. Whenever an industry standard has been available, SAA has adopted it. Whenever IBM has had to invent an interface for SAA, it has published this interface and invited the rest of the industry along.

Certainly some SAA interfaces are of little use to those with non-IBM hardware (some are of little use to those *with* IBM hardware). But this is far from "proprietary"in the sense of enslaving you to IBM forever. In fact, implementing a cooperative processing application with SAA leaves you, if anything, better able to take advantage of heterogeneous products from a wide range of vendors. If the whole industry were to standardize on such SAA components as SQL and CUA, multivendor solutions would be the norm.

## Is SAA Still in the Future?

Some developers are convinced that SAA "isn't here yet." They usually mean that some component specified in the SAA blueprint is not yet available for purchase. But these components are not SAA. SAA is a blueprint, and much of it is complete. Each forthcoming component has a place set aside for it in the overall scheme of SAA. Its position is known. Its interfaces have been specified. Only the underlying language or service that does the work is missing. It may sound strange to say "only," but once you know a component's shape, size, position, and interfaces, you know a great deal. There is no need to wait for all of SAA. Plenty of information on which to base long-term design decisions is available right now.

## SAA Evolution

Cooperative processing was not uppermost in anyone's mind when SAA was created. SAA's original agenda was, if anything, even more ambitious: standards to link not just host and workstation, but a whole range of various-sized IBM platforms. Looking at where SAA came from offers an interesting way to understand the shape it's in today and where it can take us in the future.

Almost from the moment back in the 1960s when IBM went beyond a single scalable hardware line to provide different models of computer for different market niches, SAA became more or less inevitable. By the early 1980s, widespread inconsistency among IBM platforms was causing the company huge problems, including incredible duplication of effort in software development. For just one example, a wholly separate database manager had to be written for each of the many platforms. Reducing this ruinously expensive internal logjam was the impetus behind the effort to overlay all platforms with a single common programming interface.

Widespread inconsistency was causing problems for IBM customers as well. They looked with envy at DEC customers, who had the advantage of scalable hardware, completely portable software via a common hardware instruction set, and development efforts that were highly leveraged because they could be used throughout the organization. Given IBM customers' installed base, there was no question of starting over from scratch. Nor do computers retrofit well. So IBM came up with a package of common interfaces that would let diverse platforms present a common face to the world. Enter SAA.

## *The SAA Icon Tells the Story*

The SAA icon (called "the Fireplace," probably more for its shape than for its sense of warmth and welcome) tells the story. The icon (shown in Figure 6-1) is built around a three-part core called the "software base," which predates SAA by several years. It represents the prearchitecture way of positioning a machine and its most basic software.

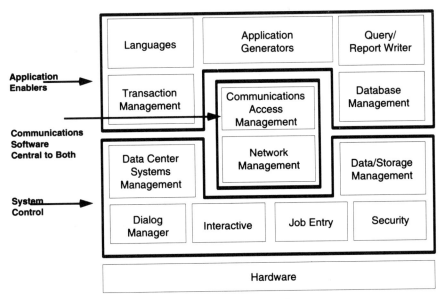

**Figure 6-4.** *SAA software base*

The software base (Figure 6-4) is hardware-specific. On top of the hardware sits a layer of System Control software that handles jobs like storage management, security, and job control; an Application Enabler layer that takes care of such things as database managers and graphics packages; and in the center are facilities for communications, communications access methods, and network management.

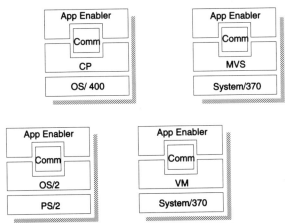

**Figure 6-5.** *Proliferation of software bases*

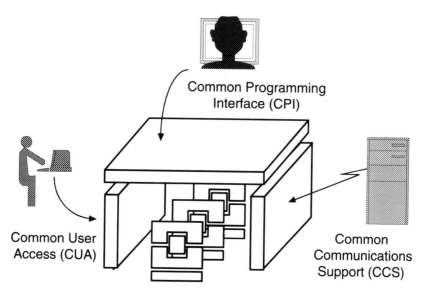

Common Programming
Interface (CPI)

Common User
Access (CUA)

Common
Communications
Support (CCS)

**Figure 6-6.** *Common layers transform software base into SAA icon*

By the middle 1980s, IBM found itself supporting a completely different software base for each hardware platform—perhaps eight or ten in
all (Figure 6-5). Many customers owned several utterly incompatible
IBM systems that they now needed to interconnect. To impose consistency in the face of such diversity, IBM decided to hide the internal
differences in platforms by building "protective walls" around them.
These layers would provide common interfaces to users, to programmers, and to other machines. From these three points of view, what lay
at the core of the system would no longer be important; every base
would be addressed in the same way. With these walls in place, the
software base now resembles the familiar Fireplace (Figure 6-6).

The SAA interfaces function something like a false front designed to
make a row of old storefronts look like a single new business. They are
equally superficial. Disguising fundamental inconsistency goes a long
way toward promoting *interoperable* systems, but tends to be insufficient for truly *portable* ones. Before applications can be picked up and
moved from platform to platform, the internals of each platform have to
be made truly similar. This is one of SAA's main agenda items for the
future. Fortunately for us, though, interoperability suits cooperative
processing fine.

▼

## THE USER'S PERSPECTIVE

While business pressures were driving IBM to develop standardized inter-faces, a concurrent evolution on the user side led to the same result by another path.

Back in 1985, a PC user ran applications serially. Whatever application was running at a given time took over the screen and imposed its own rules. The user had to adapt to each application's look, pace, and conventions. If she found two programs where F7 meant the same thing, she would be astonished at the coincidence.

Windowing fired the shot heard 'round the world. Once a user could see multiple programs on the screen simultaneously, differences in user inter-faces became intolerable. How can F7 mean "page forward" for the upper left-hand part of your screen, and "delete document" for the bottom center? There was an even more profound change. With several different products in front of her at the same time, the user now sensed that *she* owned the screen. No longer would Lotus take over her plate of glass; she would just lend them a corner of it for a while. When a user can move or resize an application window, or even zap it down to an icon, the whole power bal-ance changes. A user-driven, user-centered, consistent environment became mandatory.

As soon as most vendors standardized on the look-and-feel, user expecta-tions leapt forward again. Applications that share the screen, look similar, and behave consistently ought to be able to interact. It seems natural to pick up data from one window and move it into the document in a neighboring window. Natural, perhaps, but difficult to achieve. Exchanging data requires that applications communicate with one another down at the program level—thus, common programming interfaces become necessary. Moving data among windows eventually requires communication interfaces as well. The user may want to transfer data among applications that appear local to her PC, but in fact live 2,000 miles apart.

Thus, increased user interface consistency creates a need for program-ming interfaces, which creates a need for consistency in communication interfaces. Clearly, consistency for users, programmers, and other machines are linked in a variety of ways. Wherever the revolution starts, it doesn't stop until all three sides catch up.

## SAA's Agenda Switch

SAA first appeared promising standards strong enough to support soft-ware portability among platforms. In a nostalgic return to the days of scalable hardware, IBM envisioned programs that could be written on any SAA platform and then moved intact to another platform, recompiled, and run with little or no alteration. This promise came partly in response to the challenge from DEC, but also because program portability seemed a logical result of the sorts of standardization that SAA had in mind.

By mid-1989, portability was being mentioned less and less, and soon it disappeared from SAA literature all together. This switch in the SAA agenda had two causes. First, program portability turned out to be far more difficult to achieve than SAA architects had imagined. More important, the marketplace seemed to be less interested in portability than in interoperability—the ability of two or more programs to work cooperatively (Figure 6-7). Interoperability requires less overall architectural consistency than does portability because it deals only with the *external* interfaces of a program and not with its *internal* standards. Interoperable programs can be internally quite different as long as they are able to communicate, share files and databases, and transfer control easily between themselves.

Interoperability lays the groundwork for cooperative processing, for this is what makes it possible to distribute application logic across multiple cooperating platforms. SAA attracted most of its support from people who had the linking of host and workstation machines in mind.

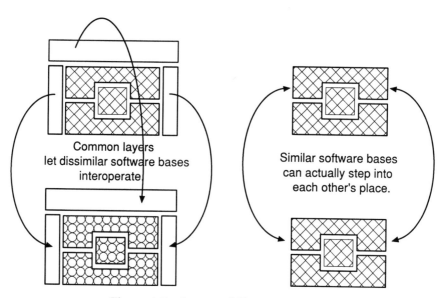

**Figure 6-7.** *Interoperability vs. portability*

Over time, even IBM came to agree (or, some say, was forced to acknowledge) that cooperative processing would be SAA's main benefit.

## Deeper into SAA

As we tour the SAA interfaces in the next three chapters, keep in mind that we are looking here at using SAA to do something it was not originally designed to do. Parts of SAA give no help at all with cooperative processing, and much of what's needed for cooperative processing is not in SAA. But there are large areas of overlapping interest.

The next few chapters aim to give developers of cooperative processing applications a clear idea of what ready-made architectural components and structures SAA provides and how much of the total standards-and-structures job it can be counted on to handle.

Developers approach SAA through the programming interface (Figure 6-8), so we examine the CPI first, even though most other books treat it as the "middle" layer. We concentrate on pointing out where the CPI is strong and where it is weak. Since the purpose of a programming interface is to hide the details of the underlying activity from the programmer, what you have to learn about the other parts of SAA will depend on how good a job the CPI does in various areas. For example, the Communications Interface piece of the CPI—the one through which programmers address the CCS—successfully masks massive amounts of complexity, so you can get away with only a cursory knowledge of the inner workings of the CCS. On the other hand, the part of the CPI through which programmers address the user interface does not work well at all, so you will have to get directly involved with the details of the CUA. If you have a good accountant, you don't have to know much about the tax code; if you have a young and inexperienced accountant, start studying those *Internal Revenue Bulletins.*

You will find, then, that:

- Our view of the **CPI** (Chapter 7) is largely evaluative. To examine everything that SAA assembles for the programmer would mean writing an encyclopedia of computing. You will have to learn about relational databases and COBOL syntax elsewhere; there are hundreds of books on these topics. The important thing is to know where you can relax and rely on the CPI and where you can't.

- **CCS** (Chapter 8) is viewed from afar. A solid and familiar interface shields developers from the internals of the communications protocols, so it is enough to look at what SAA has chosen to include,

**Figure 6-8.** *SAA from developer's point of view*

what it plans for the future, and what attitude it takes toward major movements in communications technology.

- **CUA** (Chapter 9) is treated in greater depth than either of the other layers. At this early stage in the technology, the programming interface provides little help. The interface is so thin that programmers see straight through and manipulate low-level components directly.

# 7

## Common Programming Interface (CPI)

The CPI represents the developer's view into an SAA environment. Where the CPI provides a successful programmer's interface to another part of SAA, as it does to the Common Communications layer, it saves the programmer a great deal of trouble. Where the CPI interface is weak, as it is to the Common User Access layer, it leaves the programmer largely on her own.

Like the software development field itself, SAA's CPI is on the move. This is not just a matter of new components being added; fundamental structural changes are taking place.

### CPI in Two Layers

Originally, SAA split its programming interface into two layers: CPI Languages and CPI Services. The first contained the various SAA-approved languages in which the developer could express the application he was building. The other defined standard services to be implemented on each SAA platform. The original 1987 idea was that, once these languages and services were in place across all SAA environments (OS/2, VM, MVS, AS400), applications written on any one of those environments would be portable to any of the others. Even after the agenda switch to interoperability (Chapter 6), internal IBM guidelines have continued to stipulate that no CPI element will be included in SAA unless it is implemented fully across all four platforms (excepting platforms where it would be meaningless, such as implementing a graphical user interface standard on a machine with no graphics capability).

As time has passed, the creators of SAA have come to view the application-building processes as broader than just programming. They have decided the programmer's view should encompass the whole range of activities that make up the software development lifecycle—the same range, not coincidentally, covered by today's CASE

**61**

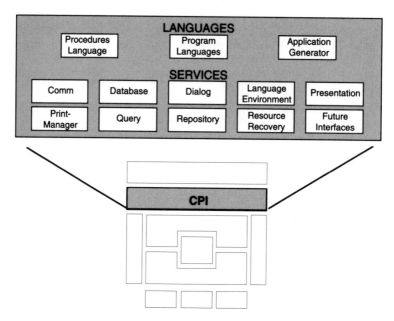

**Figure 7-1.**   *CPI "Classic"*

(Computer-Aided Software Engineering) technology. For the IBM world, CASE boils down to IBM's own AD/Cycle framework for application development, and so AD/Cycle has now gained semiofficial status as a part of the CPI. In effect, the SAA programming interface has evolved from the simple two-layer structure shown in Figure 7-1 to the complex structure-within-a-structure of Figure 7-2.

The issue of including AD/Cycle in SAA has generated extensive debate within the SAA community. Purists point out that AD/Cycle is product-oriented and thus out of place in an architectural blueprint. When SAA mentions COBOL, it means the ANSI COBOL standard; when AD/Cycle mentions COBOL, it means a specific compiler (e.g., MVS Cobol/2) that you are supposed to go out and buy. Is SAA operating here on too many levels at once?

This book is going to bow out of this debate. As SAA pragmatists, we embrace whatever tools help get these difficult cooperative applications built. Thus we devote a good chunk of this chapter to AD/Cycle and its place in the CPI. We describe both the 1987 CPI Languages layer and the augmented AD/Cycle layer (which includes languages, along with much else) that has replaced it. Then we move on to the (blessedly unchanged) CPI Services layer.

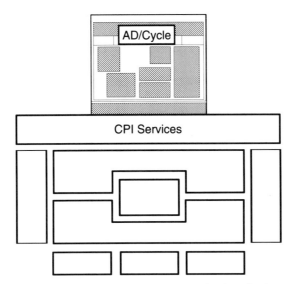

**Figure 7-2.** *AD/Cycle added to the developer's view*

## CPI Languages

Figure 7-3 shows the CPI Languages arranged in three categories: Programming Languages, Procedures Language, and Application Generator.

### *Programming Languages*

The CPI's five Programming Languages include the most popular 3GLs used in IBM environments. Note, however, that popularity is not the criterion for inclusion. Many very popular, even strategic, languages such as Ada and Pascal have been omitted, and for this reason: an SAA language must be implemented across all four platforms. To port Ada or Pascal to all SAA environments would entail a massive software project at IBM, and it hasn't seemed worth the effort.

Two of these five languages stand out as by far the most useful for cooperative processing. COBOL is the language of choice for expressing business logic across all SAA platforms. Since COBOL has an installed base of three million programmers and 90 billion lines of code, this is no surprise. For workstation platforms, C is the preferred language.

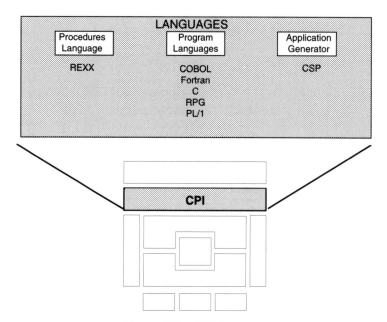

**Figure 7-3.** *CPI Languages*

### Procedures Language

SAA Procedures Language is based on REXX and is quite useful for a variety of jobs. Its original charter was to provide a standardized command language after the fashion of CLISTs, EXECs, and JCL. While it does well in that context, it also serves as an "embedded" language. An embedded language is almost the opposite of a command language; instead of being on the "outside" of an application, it is on the "inside" where it can add user-programmable logic to a product. For example, IBM's Query Manager uses a REXX subset as an embedded language for its procedures.

### Application Generator

The Application Generator is SAA's name for IBM's Cross-System Product (CSP). It is sometimes described as a 4GL, but actually it is more like a 3½GL. Originally designed for building simple on-line applications, it tends to be highly screen-oriented, which is not a useful attribute for cooperative processing applications. Recent enhancements have increased portability, provided an input for CASE tools (External

Source Format, or ESF), and greatly increased speed in some environments. In the long term, it seems likely that the Application Generator will make its biggest contribution to cooperative processing not as a stand-alone tool but in its generator role in AD/Cycle.

## AD/Cycle

In September of 1989, IBM announced AD/Cycle, its long-awaited CASE framework. AD/Cycle represented a stunning change of direction for IBM, for it included other vendors' products alongside IBM's own and was in fact designed in consultation with these other vendors.

Just as SAA is represented by the "Fireplace" diagram, AD/Cycle has its "eight blocks of granite" icon, shown in Figure 7-4. Each block represents a slot for products that deal with some aspect of software development. (The rectangles with italicized print are not blocks, but are just labels that indicate in what development phase the blocks fall.) A brief look at each of the eight blocks will give a good idea of what AD/Cycle actually contains.

### *Application Development Platform*

The bottom block of the diagram spans all phases of the development process and represents basic shared facilities for all the tools. Some of

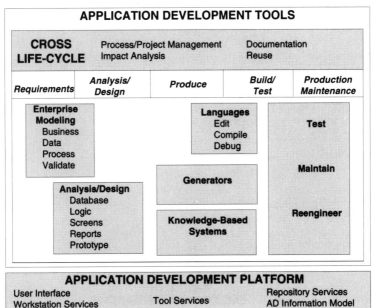

**Figure 7-4.** *AD/Cycle's "eight blocks of granite"*

these components provide common services for user interface, work station connectivity, and Repository access (the Repository is the database in which AD/Cycle stores detailed information about the development process), as well as that crucial template for Repository organization known as the Information Model (IM).

The IM is the soul of AD/Cycle. Looking at the dozens—soon to be hundreds—of products integrating with AD/Cycle, you wonder how all of these disparate tools will work together on an activity that the end user needs to perceive as a seamless development process. Making this happen is the job of the IM.

The IM defines the vocabulary of CASE tools. It is a highly structured vocabulary, defining whole networks of concepts. The basic idea is that once CASE tools share the same structured vocabulary, they can inter-communicate with each other, passing specifications, designs, dia-grams, working code, even documentation, from tool to tool. The IM uses data modeling techniques to describe the software development process. The IM is not cast in concrete; individual tools or groups of tools can extend the vocabulary in unanticipated ways. There is a catch here, though: to the extent that the model is modified for a special purpose, other tools cannot uniformly tie into its functionality.

### Enterprise Modeling

The products in the Enterprise Modeling block help a business under-stand and model its process and data requirements. Some meth-odologies call this the "requirements-gathering" phase of a project, but it actually seems more comprehensive than that. Enterprise Modeling tools can be used to describe how the business works even independent of any computer system that may need to be developed. Once the busi-ness is more fully understood, it will presumably be clear what new activities—possibly computerized, possibly not—the business needs to undertake.

### Analysis and Design

As requirements emerge from the Enterprise Modeling phase, Analysis and Design tools help convert them into application design specifica-tions. The tools in this block support such techniques as entity-relation-ship (ER) diagrams, data-flow diagrams, and structure charts.

Here, as in other phases of AD/Cycle, tools should be directly "Repository-enabled" so that they can write to and read from the

Repository. Once enabled, an Analysis/Design tool can read the Modeling output directly, and the designs it produces can in turn be picked up by the next step, the "Produce" phase tools that might build the system.

### Languages, Generators, and Knowledge-Based Systems

The three different blocks in the Produce phase of AD/Cycle represent the different levels of language development. The Languages block supports the various SAA 3GL languages. The Knowledge-Based Systems (KBS) block will eventually support knowledge-based systems that can be integrated with other Produce phase components. The Generators block needs more explanation.

A big problem with the Generators block is its name. As new products are added, this block seems to have less and less to do with generating anything. It is really just a container for higher-level languages— languages that can dramatically increase productivity and decrease code bulk. Sometimes the eponymous code generator produces 3GL from a high-level syntax; more often, the language directly executes or even compiles the syntax. A better name for this block might be "Environments," because higher-level constructs usually get their leverage by executing in a specialized environment that has extra knowledge about databases, user interfaces, or whatever their particular product does.

### Test, Maintenance, and Redevelopment Tools

The products in the farthest right-hand block in the diagram operate on systems that have already been built. These products perform a variety of functions, including mainframe application testing from workstation scripts, test data coverage analysis, COBOL structured programming aid, and system reengineering.

### Cross Life Cycle Tools

The last of the eight blocks spans the top of the AD/Cycle diagram. The products it contains apply throughout the application development life cycle. These include project management tools (for tracking and planning projects), impact analysis tools (for analyzing the effects of change on software), and process management tools (for designing and managing the very process of software development).

This last deserves special mention. AD/Cycle is often accused of enforcing the so-called "waterfall" methodology, with projects proceeding inexorably in one direction, from Analysis to Design to Build to Test to Maintain. The layout of the blocks-of-granite diagram can reinforce this sense of left-to-right progression. In fact, though, the top layer allows you to customize your development process, to *program* a methodology. This methodology might be iterative, so that at any point you can go back and repeat steps until the result is acceptable, and then proceed to the next step. Or you might choose a reengineering methodology in which the last block (Test/Maintain/Reengineer) is tied to the first block and fed back into the enterprise model. The reengineering approach reinforces the philosophy that software systems produce results that force the enterprise to change its view of its business, which in turn drives the software to change, and so on.

Cross Life Cycle's process management component, then, is the glue that finally holds the AD/Cycle pieces together in the developer's eyes and provides the methodology he will use throughout the development process.

## CPI Services

Compared to the top half of the CPI, the lower-level Services sublayer has stayed remarkably stable, changing only as new services have been added.

The following sections summarize the current Common Services. Each service is defined, its importance evaluated, and its relationship to the SAA application shown with a diagram. We do not include the actual application program interface (API) definitions because they are thoroughly documented elsewhere. Also, these definitions sometimes assume familiarity with major sections of technology, such as relational databases or SNA, which lead far beyond the scope of this book.

Each interface gets a "CP grade" that expresses its usefulness for cooperative processing (from A, very useful, to C, not useful). When two scores are separated by an arrow, it means that the value is changing; A → C means the value is dropping from very useful to not useful. Note that this ranking is not a general evaluation of the service, but only of its usefulness within a cooperative processing context.

### Communications Interface (CP Grade: B → A)

The Communications Interface (CI, widely called CPIC, pronounced like "civic" with a *p*) provides the basic methods by which two peer

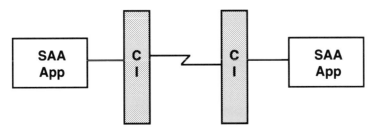

**Figure 7-5.** *Communications Interface*

SAA applications connect and communicate with each other. CI (Figure 7-5) supports an architected API for SNA's Logical Unit Type 6.2 (LU6.2) peer-to-peer communication protocol. LU6.2 has been implemented on many environments, both IBM and non-IBM. As we will see in a subsequent section, it can be pressed into service to create client/ server as well as peer-to-peer interactions.

Since this is the only CPI interface that currently implements communications, you might expect a straight A in CP usefulness. It got the early B because, for a long time, it was not *implemented* in several useful environments. Only very recently has CI been implemented in OS/2, OS/400, and MVS. But even when it was just a blueprint, CI had grade-B usefulness to those of us who were building SAA applications in 1988. The blueprint helped plug the hole in the architecture and give a CI look to the caulking.

### Database Interface (CP Grade: A)

SAA's Database Interface (DBI, Figure 7-6) is the single most important interface in the CPI. Its job is to provide the SAA application with an architected interface to the database. The interface language is SQL,

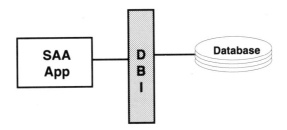

**Figure 7-6.** *Database Interface*

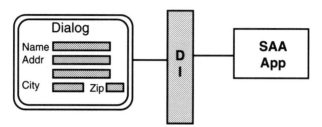

**Figure 7-7.** *Dialog Interface*

the industry standard for database access. SQL's success comes from ties to the relational database model, with its superior ease-of-use and ability to support multiple logical views on a single database (so that different departments can view the same data in different ways).

Virtually every cooperative processing system in existence uses SQL in some important way. We will see in the upcoming design section that a whole category of cooperative systems depends on SQL's distributed capabilities. If anything, SQL may be somewhat overused in places where other approaches would be superior.

### Dialog Interface (CP Grade: B → C)

As an SAA cooperative processing interface, the Dialog Interface (DI) was killed off before it got going. The DI (Figure 7-7) supports the mainframe style of user interface—system-driven panels (what we call "Formatted Screens" in the CUA chapter). This style has been implemented under ISPF on TSO, under EZ-VU on DOS, and Dialog Manager on OS/2. While appropriate for mainframe/terminal levels of interaction, it fails to exploit the power of the intelligent workstation's graphical environment. Even so, DI proponents have argued, this style deserved a place on the workstation, if only to promote migration from and consistency with mainframe applications. Nevertheless, in mid-1990, IBM announced that Dialog extensions were being halted and that other tools should be used to build graphical user interfaces.

The Dialog Interface retains some usefulness for host-driven terminal dialogs. But it has essentially been abandoned as an SAA interface and should not be used for cooperative processing systems.

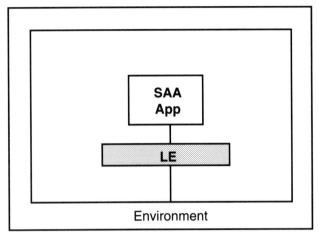

**Figure 7-8.** *Language Environment*

## Language Environment (CP Grade: B → A)

As we write, the SAA Language Environment (LE) has just appeared. LE (Figure 7-8) supports a "standard library" of language services that span all the SAA machines and languages. Services include a language-independent capability to handle the tricky case of "exceptions" (such as system or software failures), standardized message services for informational or diagnostic messages, storage management (heap and stack) that can be shared by multiple languages, and various math and date routines. These services may seem trivial, but they handle some of the stickier problems of building applications that span multiple platforms. As LE services become widely installed, they should prove their usefulness.

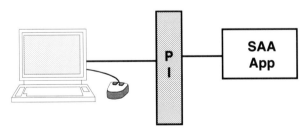

**Figure 7-9.** *Presentation Interface*

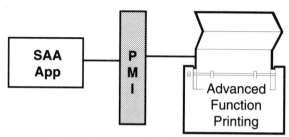

**Figure 7-10.** *PrintManager Interface*

## Presentation Interface (CP Grade: A → B)

The SAA Presentation Interface (PI, Figure 7-9) furnishes the API to the OS/2 Presentation Manager. It is one of the few CPIs with platform constraints: it will not be implemented anywhere but OS/2. The PI is a huge interface. By the time you count up the hundreds of "calls" in the API and then add in the messages that can be sent, you'll find nearly one thousand ways of invoking PI. It rivals in complexity its cousin, the Microsoft Windows API.

Since user interface (UI) development paradigms are at still an early stage of evolution, PI is quite primitive and clumsy to use. Rather than programming in what is little more than a "UI Assembler," developers should turn to higher-grade tools. PI was the only choice for graphical cooperative processing systems back in 1988, but now we can relegate it to building special-purpose UI components.

## PrintManager Interface (CP Grade: B → A)

The relatively new PrintManager Interface (PMI) will expand its usefulness as it gets implemented more widely. PMI (Figure 7-10) solves one of the uglier problems in distributed systems: how to get something printed regardless of the type of document or the type of network printer. Alas, PMI can't fully solve these kinds of problems because printer support varies so widely (fonts, images, color, etc). Still, it will greatly improve upon what we have now.

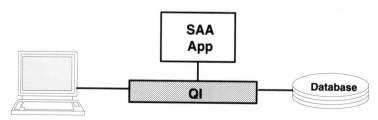

**Figure 7-11.** *Query Interface*

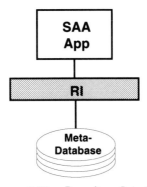

**Figure 7-12.** *Repository Interface*

### Query Interface (CP Grade: B)

The Query Interface (QI, Figure 7-11) provides a standardized interface to the IBM Query Manager product, which supports direct query access to the SAA relational databases. Although most cooperative processing systems get along without the QI, it provides a nice service for those that need it. QI gives programmers a quick way to build forms, procedures, or reports, but cooperative systems will probably require far richer interfaces than forms can provide. QI will prove most valuable for generating standard sort-and-break reports with a minimum of development work.

### Repository Interface (CP Grade: C)

The Repository Interface (RI, Figure 7-12), while powerful, gets a low CP grade because it is not relevant for today's cooperative processing systems. The RI is the API into the MVS/Repository Manager, providing access into the AD/Cycle meta-database. RI is primarily of interest to builders of CASE tools. Note that, like PI, it has a platform constraint, though the opposite one: RI will be implemented on all platforms *except* OS/2.

The RI may earn a higher grade in the future, as sophisticated cooperative processing systems start accessing the Repository directly—to look up system message formats, for example.

### Resource Recovery Interface (CP Grade: B → A)

This smallest of the CPI interfaces may hold the most future promise. Resource Recovery Interface (RRI, Figure 7-13) implements only two

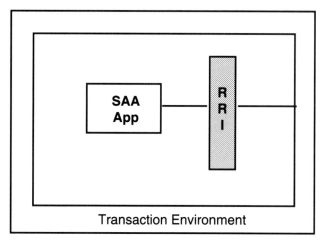

**Figure 7-13.** *Resource Recovery Interface*

calls: SRRCMIT (Commit) and SRRBACK (Backout), standard APIs for
signaling to the transaction management environment that we wish to
commit changes or to roll them back out. While RRI is currently implemented only in IMS/TM and VM, it will spread to the other SAA transaction managers. Its future involves even more interesting plans to
control commitment across multiple systems. This is a tall order requiring "two phase commit" protocols that can span SAA environments.
Such an implementation will solve many difficult problems in distributed transaction processing, but swift implementation is unlikely.

# 8

# Common Communications Support (CCS)

CCS establishes the rules that allow systems to talk to one another under SAA. CCS is actually composed of numerous communication protocol definitions, a protocol being an agreement between two cooperating processes that governs their interactions.

We have almost overtaken our own definition of architecture here. By its very nature, the communications discipline has required more architecture earlier than has any other part of the industry. This is why the CCS side of SAA is by far the most mature. When SAA was first announced, its communications interface consisted of protocols that were already fully formed and well established. (This does not mean that CCS has been static; powerful industry forces are driving evolution in communications as fast as in any of the other areas.)

The programming interface to CCS works very well, and so the developer has fairly minimal exposure to the communications protocols themselves. This chapter simply reviews the contents of the CCS and points out some important issues implicit in the CCS organization and evolution.

## CCS Organization

There are currently about thirty separate protocols in CCS, with every indication that the number will keep growing. Many people wonder why there are so many. Isn't there a single standard way to connect two processors, like the impulses that connect two telephones?

In fact, the telephone provides a good basis for understanding this multiplicity. When you think about it, phone communication happens in many different ways. There may be copper wiring between your home phone and the central phone office, but central offices may connect with each other by microwave or fiber. The protocol for a voice conversation over the phone is built around the grammar of human language and the

intonations of the human voice; but answering machines, voice mail systems, fax machines, modems, and burglar alarms all communicate over
phone lines using quite different sets of standards and signals. In the
same way, multiple CCS protocols are needed to deal with various
issues: how points connect, how they network with other machines, how
they represent various data formats, how they provide security.

## SNA and OSI

For each of these connections, SAA's CCS contains a double set of protocols, as Figure 8-1 shows. Largely for marketplace reasons, CCS has
chosen to support not only IBM's own SNA-protocol stacks, but the

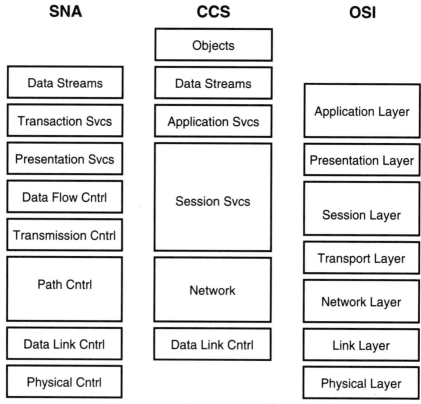

**Figure 8-1.** *Three communication stacks*

open-standards-based Open Systems Interconnect (OSI) model as well. OSI complicates CCS diagrams, but it reflects IBM's growing commitment to interconnecting its environments with the rest of the world's.

Both the SNA- and OSI-protocol stacks are structured as layered architectures. A layered architecture stacks individual protocols on top of each other, from the low-level protocols that deal with highly detailed issues of communication activity up to higher-level protocols that deal with increasingly general levels of semantic content. Layering protocols this way makes it possible to deal with several different categories of concerns (that is, layers) without confusing the individual issues that each layer introduces.

▼

## THE TWO PHILOSOPHERS

In a 1981 article, Andrew S. Tanenbaum uses a three-layer analogy, illustrated in Figure 8-2, to explain how multilayer communication works:

> Consider the problem of the two talking philosophers. Philosopher 1 lives in an ivory tower in Kenya and speaks only Swahili. Philosopher 2 lives in a cave in India and speaks only Telugu. Nevertheless, Philosopher 1 wishes to convey his affection for *Oryctolagaus cuniculus* to his Indian colleague (the philosophers are layer 3 peers). Since the philosophers speak different languages, each engages the services of a translator (layer 2 process) and an engineer (layer 1 process).
>
> To convey his thoughts, Philosopher 1 passes his message, in Swahili, to his translator, across the 3/2 interface. The translator may convert it to English, French, Dutch, or some other language, depending only on the layer 2 protocol. The translator then hands his output to his engineer across the 2/1 interface for transmission. The physical mode of transmission may be telegram, telephone, computer network, or something else, depending only on the layer 1 protocol. When the Indian engineer receives the message, he passes it to his translator for rendition into Telugu. Finally, the Indian translator gives the message, in Telugu, to his philosopher.
>
> This analogy illustrates three points. First, each person thinks of his communication as being primarily horizontal with his peer (although in reality it is vertical, except in layer 1). For example, Philosopher 1 regards himself as conversing with Philosopher 2, even though his only physical communication is with translator 1. Second, actual communication is vertical, not horizontal, except in layer 1. Third, the three protocols are completely independent. The philosophers can switch the subject from rabbits to guinea pigs at will; the translators can switch from English to Dutch at will; the engineers can switch from telegram to telephone at will. The peers in any layer can change their protocol without affecting the other layers. It is for precisely this reason that networks are designed as a series of layers—to prevent changes in one part of the design (e.g., caused by technological advances) from requiring changes in other parts.

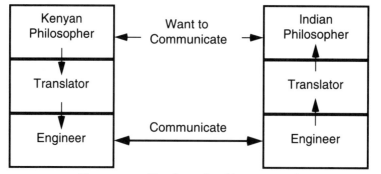

**Figure 8-2.** *How layered architectures work*

(Andrew S. Tanenbaum, "Network Protocols," *Computing Surveys* (December 1981), pages 453-489. Copyright 1981, Association for Computing Machinery, Inc.)

## Protocols

The thirty or so protocols contained in CCS are divided among six broad layers. A brief description of each, moving from the top layer down, follows.

### Object Content Architectures

The Object Content Architecture layer contains a variety of protocols that describe how complex data objects are represented. These include:

- Printer-ready text (PTOCA).
- Images (IOCA).
- Fonts (FOCA).
- Graphics (GOCA).
- Data formats used for data sharing among heterogeneous database management systems (FD:OCA).

### Data Streams

The Data Stream layer defines the formats for ordered streams of data elements with a variety of uses. These include data streams for:

- All-points-addressable printers (IPDS).
- Nonprogrammable terminals (3270DS).

- Word processing documents (RFT:DCA).
- Compound object documents (MO:DCA).
- Multiple character set data (CDRA).

### Application Services

Application Services defines protocols used by networked applications to provide numerous standardized services. These protocols include:

- Electronic envelopes for document interchange (DIA).
- Store-and-forward delivery services (SNA/DS).
- A generalized protocol for network and systems management (SNA/MS).
- A distributed file system (DDM).
- Interconnecting distributed relational databases (DRDA), probably the most significant of the protocols.

Application Services also supports OSI Application Layer protocols for electronic mail (X.400) and network file management (FTAM).

### Session Services

A session is a logical connection between two SAA systems that endures across many back-and-forth messages. Session Services are provided by the centerpiece protocol of CCS: SNA LU6.2. LU6.2 defines the formats and protocols for a general-purpose program-to-program communication. Where more primitive communication protocols focused on how a program would connect to some remote device, such as a dumb terminal or printer, LU6.2 assumes intelligence and programmability at both ends. This makes LU6.2 especially appropriate as devices of all types become intelligent and as systems become increasingly distributed.

Session Services also includes three OSI layers: Presentation, Session, and Transport.

### Network Services

Network Services are the protocols required to connect two SAA systems directly through intermediate nodes. This SNA protocol is called Low-Entry Networking (LEN) or Physical Unit Type 2.1 (PU T2.1). OSI support comes via the OSI Network layer.

### Data Link Control

Data Link Control is the lowest CCS layer. It provides the basic ability to connect two points together reliably. Three types of data links are supported:

- SNA's SDLC.
- X.25 in packed-switched data networks.
- Token-ring LANs.

Just recently, Integrated Services Data Network (ISDN) has been added to CCS. ISDN is attracting worldwide interest as a uniform communications vehicle for data, voice, facsimile, and video. One day a single ISDN cable into our home or business will take care of all communications needs.

### Protocol Relationships

Notice that these six layers of protocols build upon one another. Higher-level concerns call upon the services of lower-level concerns. For example, an Application Service like a DIA electronic envelope invokes LU6.2 to ship the message that sits on PU T2.1 nodes delivering data over a token-ring.

### Observations about CCS

An excursion into the world of communications can frighten even the most seasoned technician. Rather than getting bogged down among formats and protocols, developers of cooperative processing applications can get by with a few general observations about CCS.

- **CCS is targeted at distributed systems:** Despite a few concessions to the past (notably the 3270 data stream), CCS promotes those forms of connectivity that suit rich distributed systems: program-to-program messaging, distributed files, even distributed databases. These protocols anticipate highly distributed intelligence in future peer-to-peer networks.

- **CCS is surprisingly "open":** Industry analysts have been surprised at the degree to which SAA has embraced the industry-controlled OSI protocols alongside its own SNA protocols. In fact, the very nomenclature of the CCS layers ("Application, "Session," "Network") comes from the OSI protocol stacks.

Some people seem disturbed that IBM has addressed the differences between SNA and OSI standards by "simply" adopting both. Systems executives are not among these people. These executives need the higher-performance, superior network-managed SNA to solve today's problems, and they also need OSI to connect to the growing UNIX and international communities. SAA's attempt at combining the two within CCS makes a lot of pragmatic sense.

- **The better CCS gets, the less you will see of it:** As technology—and communications technology in particular—gets better, it becomes less visible. CCS already does a good job of hiding itself from the developer. As new features come along—ISDN support, for example—they should be able to hide themselves under LU6.2, which is in turn hidden by the CPI Communication Interface. Ideally, the developer will deal only with issues of how his particular application needs to work. Communications becomes the wiring behind the wallboard behind the paint, invisibly providing the services needed to build cooperative processing applications.

# 9

# *Common User Access (CUA)*

User interface architectures are quite new to the world. Few developers have as much experience in this area as they have in programming languages or communications. Communications have been architected for 20 years; programming languages and services for at least 10; but not until 1987, with the announcement of SAA, has there been such a thing as an architecture for user interfaces. Everyone is still at the beginning of the learning curve.

SAA did not invent user interface technology, by any means (in fact, SAA has only just caught up to acceptable industry levels). But SAA did contribute the *architecture* part. Previously, advanced UI projects at Xerox, Apple, Microsoft, Metaphor, and elsewhere treated user interfaces casually, with "style guides" that summarized whatever practices had evolved around their particular products. SAA, aiming at a *multiproduct* UI style guide, had to start further back and create an underlying set of principles and standards. For the first time, formal architecture came to this improvisational area of computing.

For all its high ambition, SAA's programming interface to the CUA is quite primitive and spotty. As with all new technologies, coming up with a succinct, standard interface takes time.

UI programming stands roughly where database programming stood 15 years ago, before SQL came along. Back then, each database management system (DBMS)—System 2000, Total, DL/1, for instance—had a dramatically different programming interface, each with dozens of different calls. Even worse, each rested upon a different underlying data model. Programmers had to understand thoroughly the syntax and the semantics of any DBMS they planned to address and tailor a separate application for each one. This confusion lasted until the triumph of the relational data model—along with SQL, its access language—gave programmers a standard and simple way to access any data from almost any adhering database product.

There is no SQL-equivalent yet for user interfaces. OS2/PM, Windows, Motif, OpenLook, and other UI environments continue to experiment and compete. Each has different APIs and semantics, with no cross-system standard in sight. Object-oriented user interfaces (OOUI, discussed later in this chapter) loom on the horizon as the potential "relational databases" of UI, but they remain some distance off. In the meantime, programmers need, again, to understand thoroughly the syntax and semantics of whatever UI they will be working with.

## CUA and Cooperative Processing

CUA plays an unheralded and unique role within SAA. This is the interface that really injects the notion of cooperative processing into SAA.

As we have said, cooperative processing, while now an integral part of the SAA agenda, shows up nowhere in the formal structure of SAA itself. While the CPI and CCS seem to contain several interfaces that are *sympathetic* to cooperative processing, even more of their interfaces seem to point toward a centralized, mainframe-only architecture.

CUA, however, tips the balance decisively toward cooperative processing. CUA requires powerful, graphical user interfaces, which are achievable only on workstation machines. So any "centralized, mainframe-only" SAA application written for SAA's VM, MVS, or OS/400 platforms has to link up with an OS/2 machine in order to present the user interface that CUA demands. The result: a circuitous but inescapable prescription for cooperative processing.

## What Is a UI Architecture Made Of?

What does this new and crucial creature, a UI architecture, look like? It is considerably less rigid than other kinds of architectures because one component of the system is a human, and humans don't tend to be as architectable as machines. The components of a UI architecture even have a humane sound: look, feel, and paradigm.

### Look-and-Feel

Look-and-feel, the subject of highly publicized lawsuits between software companies, is the obvious feature of a user interface. "Look"—which CUA calls the Presentation Language—refers to what the user sees: color, graphical elements, windows, icons, scrollbars, characters, fonts, cursors, dialog boxes, and other presentation elements. "Feel"—

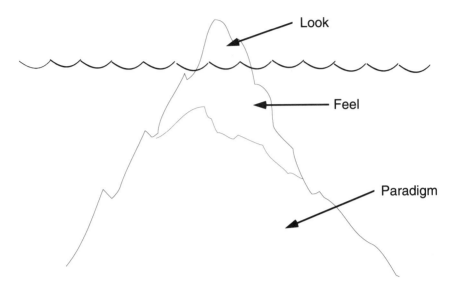

**Figure 9-1.** *More to a user interface than look-and-feel*

which CUA calls the Interaction Language—describes how the user controls, responds to, or interacts with what is on the screen. This could mean typing on a keyboard, hitting various key combinations, moving a mouse, or even pointing at a touch-sensitive screen.

### Paradigm

The look and the feel are the visible (strictly speaking—the visible and *tangible*) parts of the user interface. An even bigger part (Figure 9-1) looms beneath the surface, one that even the lawyers haven't figured out how to name and copyright. We call this the user interface "paradigm." It is, in CUA's words, the interface's Process Sequence. CUA classifies UI paradigms as either action-object or object-action and clearly specifies the object-action paradigm for advanced new systems.

### Action-Object

An action-object paradigm takes the form of an imperative sentence: verb followed by its object. You will recognize the classical command-driven interfaces that have been used almost since the beginning of computing. MS-DOS, TSO, and CMS interactions all follow this familiar form:

> print file1 file2 file3
> backup file1 file2 file3
> erase file1 file2 file3

Action-object is not confined to command interfaces. Many menuing systems (ISPF under TSO is an example) are organized this way, allowing the user first to graphically select the action to be performed—say, choosing "Print" from a menu of commands—and then prompting her for the files to be printed.

### Object-Action

An object-action paradigm inverts the sequence. In an object-action interface, the user first selects the object or objects he is interested in and then specifies the action that he wants done to or with them. This assumes an environment where objects are presented for his selection, as on the Macintosh, in Windows or OS/2 Presentation Manager, or a "DOS Shell" like XTree.

To produce the same results as in the print-backup-erase example above, an object-action sequence would look like this:

1. User marks fileA, fileB, fileC (perhaps by clicking on their icons or filenames on the screen).
2. User chooses the action items Print, Backup, then Erase (via a pull-down menu).

At first glance this may seem like a trivial change in interaction syntax, hardly comparable to the hidden mass of an iceberg. It takes some time to appreciate how significant and fundamental a shift in relationship between user and system it implies.

While the traditional action-object paradigm places the user in a task-oriented world where the object of those tasks is in a sense secondary, object-action transforms the world into an object-oriented place. The user can scan a whole constellation of objects, select those that interest her, bring those objects to the foreground, and then decide what actions to perform on them. The nature of the chosen objects limits the possible actions to those that are appropriate: if the user selects a number of graphic objects in a "Draw" program, he will not be offered the options to "spell check," "recalculate," or "change margins."

CUA insists on the action-object paradigm for its more advanced interface levels. An interface built around objects, with actions following along, has seemed to CUA architects the best way of modeling, for both user and programmer, the way the world really works.

## CUA Consistency

If look, feel, and paradigm are the stuff from which a UI architecture is made, consistency is its first principle. Humans do not respond to highly detailed, precisely specified interfaces, but they do respond to highly consistent ones. Internal consistency makes a system easier to learn in depth, because, as Aristotle said, "We learn about things we don't know by comparing them to things we do know." Users feel free to explore new features of a system when they can count on these new features behaving like the old ones.

CUA prescribes consistency at several levels:

- **Physical consistency** governs the physical properties of the user's devices: keyboard layout, screen resolution, or mouse button arrangement, for example.

- **Syntactic consistency** prescribes usage that should remain constant: function key assignment, menu usage, window buttons that maximize and minimize, etc.

- **Semantic consistency** means that user interface elements maintain a consistent meaning. The "trash can" icon, for example, always discards things. If a user dumps a disk file icon in the trash, the file will be deleted; if she dumps a system printer icon in the trash, the printer will be deconfigured. In significantly different contexts, the function—discarding things—stays consistent.

## CUA Design Principles

CUA is built upon a few powerful design principles. Some of them have been around the user interface community for some time; others are CUA originals.

### *Is Rule-Based Rather than Tool-Based*

Recent pre-CUA user interface technology was based on tools rather than on principles. CUA has had to establish underlying rules because it intends to implement the same architecture on multiple user-interface platforms (including Windows, OSF/Motif, and others) and can accommodate such diversity only via some general principles. Furthermore, user interface technology is growing at such a rapid pace that a technology built around today's tools risks early obsolescence. Deeper analysis into the relationships between humans and objects tends to have more staying power.

### Uses Metaphors

Renaissance philosophers defined a metaphor as a "short myth." Myths and metaphors are basic ways that humans understand the universe they live in. Incorporating metaphor into user interface can make the human-computer dyad much more effective.

Dumping an unwanted object into the trash is a near-archetypal experience. So is realizing an hour later that it was actually something you needed and rooting around in the trash for it. So is scribbling notes in a book margin, or sticking a Post-It note onto a spreadsheet. CUA recognizes that user interfaces more semantically consistent with the real world get us closer to computers that are truly extensions of the user.

### Avoids Modes

A "mode" is a special state in a program that has different interface rules from the rest of the program. For example, some text editors or database editors have an *input mode,* during which anything that is typed is entered directly into the system, and which requires an "Escape" to return to the main system. Similarly, most graphical "Paint" programs have modes for special graphical entry where any mouse move leaves a thick trail of "wet paint" on the screen; escaping out returns the mouse to a standard pointer.

Some programs require modes, but fewer than was thought 10 years ago. Modes break consistency rules because actions tend to have different results within the mode than without, so CUA advocates keeping modes to a minimum.

### Encourages Forgiving Interfaces

CUA encourages, and provides syntax for, "Undo" commands. An Undo reverses actions, sometimes even expensive or consequential actions, in the interface. Undo commands let a user learn by trying, since she is protected from inadvertent catastrophes and can always find her way back from any odd byways she may have wandered into.

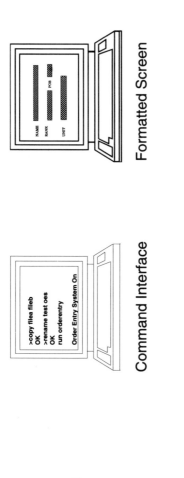

**Formatted Screen**

NAME
RANK  POB
UNIT

**Command Interface**

>copy filea fileb
OK
>rename test oes
OK
run orderentry

Order Entry System On

**Object-Oriented User Interface**

**Graphical User Interface**

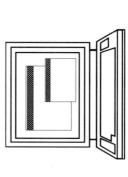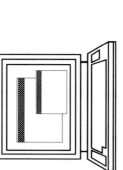

**Physical Objects**

**Character User Interface**

NAME
RANK
UNIT

**Figure 9-2.** *User interfaces move away from objects and back again*

88

## CUA Evolution

CUA has been evolving ever since SAA was announced. User interface technology is changing fast, and CUA keeps sharpening up its specifications. It is best to understand CUA evolution in the context of user interface evolution in general. Figure 9-2 shows six stages of evolution—two of them pre-CUA, and one of these even precomputer.

Eons before the first CUA documentation, long before there were such disciplines as human factors and ergonomics, the only "user interface" around was humans interacting with the things around them. Through many low-tech centuries, the **physical interface** has reached a high degree of evolution, as the computer field is only now beginning to appreciate. There is a great deal of accumulated wisdom embodied in the way people and organizations design, choose, arrange, and use physical objects. A person's desktop, for example, is covered with a selection of tools—pencils, ledgers, a stapler, a clock, some file folders—arranged in a way that suits the individual's working style. The genius of the physical desktop, with its innate object-action paradigm, is how it adapts itself to the psyche of the individual user.

Computers sped up and expanded upon the work that people had been doing with such tools as pencils, ledgers, and staples, but they were unable to mimic any of the visual, tactile, or behavioral features of these tools. Early computers were just very large calculators with converted teletypes wired on to let human beings issue instructions in the form of terse imperative statements. This style of interaction, the **command interface,** has endured for decades and persists in many of today's commercial operating systems. Making a virtue of a necessity, "computer experts" promoted this massively serial, procedure-driven interface style as the modern, streamlined way of thinking about work. Users would get used to it over time, they said. But how comfortable could users ever get with a style so skewed toward how calculators work and away from how humans work?

Ten years ago, then, a person swiveling in a chair from her desktop to her computer had to make a major shift in mind-set. Fortunately, user interface philosophy has come around since then. Recent developments in computer user interfaces can be seen as attempts to bring the computer interface back closer to the world of physical objects. Consider the next four stages:

- **Formatted screens** put what looked like a real paper form up on the terminal's plate of glass for users to fill out.
- The **character user interface,** taking advantage of the PC's ability to put local intelligence behind a user interface, introduced the dynamic object-action paradigm.

- The **graphical user interface** acknowledged users' visual capacity with graphics actually designed to be intuitive and attractive.
- The **object-oriented user interface** of the near future turns these graphics into metaphors—those infinitely powerful and expandable little pieces of human mythology and insight.

CUA acknowledges—and in many cases it helped pioneer—these most recent four stages of user interface development. It is worth looking at each in some detail.

### Formatted Screen Interface (CUA Entry Model)

The video display terminal that replaced the old teletype input made possible the formatted screen interface (Figure 9-3) that has been so widely implemented in commercial systems. It takes advantage of the whole rectangular plate of glass on a terminal screen, with a visual interface that looks like a business form. Complex objects such as sales order forms work infinitely better "shown" in a formatted screen environment than "specified" in a command interface environment.

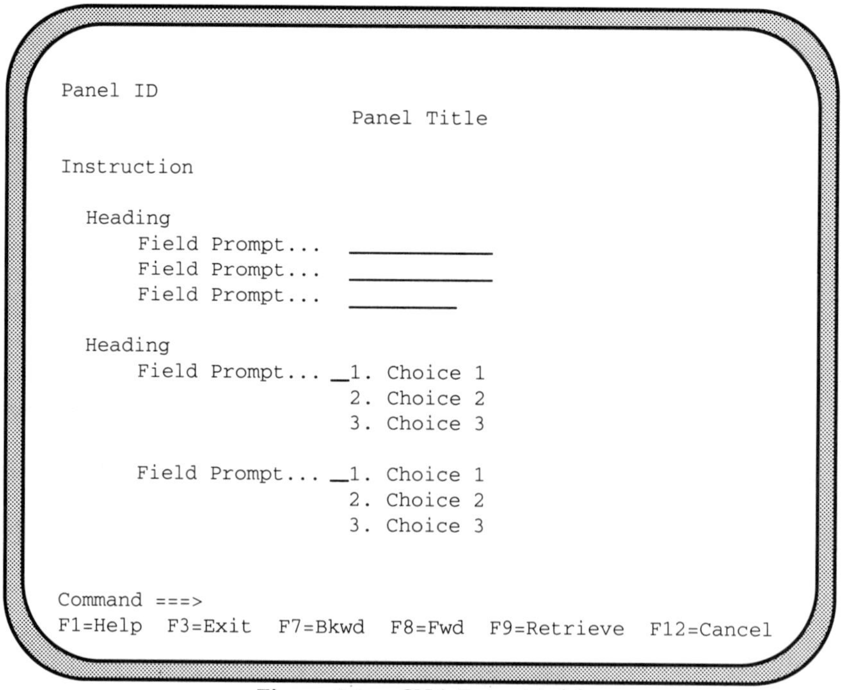

```
Panel ID
                        Panel Title

Instruction

   Heading
        Field Prompt...    _____
        Field Prompt...    _____
        Field Prompt...    _____

   Heading
        Field Prompt... _1. Choice 1
                         2. Choice 2
                         3. Choice 3

        Field Prompt... _1. Choice 1
                         2. Choice 2
                         3. Choice 3

Command ===>
F1=Help  F3=Exit  F7=Bkwd  F8=Fwd  F9=Retrieve  F12=Cancel
```

**Figure 9-3.** *CUA Entry Model*

Usually these "forms" are embedded as leaves in a tree of menus that present the user with options for various actions. Thus, formatted screen applications are more user-friendly than command interfaces, but they are still profoundly action-object systems.

CUA calls this interface style the Entry Model. The Entry Model gets people started with user interface architecture and consistency in a way that accommodates their existing equipment. Key issues for the Entry Model are:

- Panel components and layout (CUA calls formatted screens "panels").
- Basic field types and behavior.
- The way commands are given to the system.
- Function key conventions and usage.
- Handling and presentation of scrollable areas.
- Help and Message conventions.

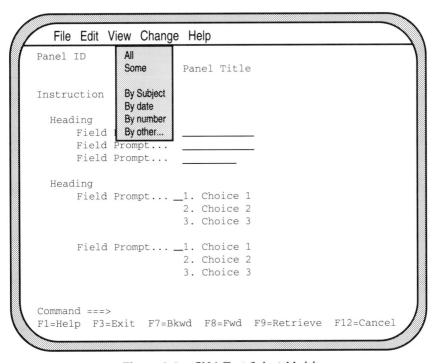

**Figure 9-4.** *CUA Text Subset Model*

### Character User Interface (CUA Text Subset Model)

As we have seen, PC technology revolutionized user interfaces. With more computing horsepower brought right to the keyboard and display, vastly more interesting interfaces become possible.

The character user interface (CUI), shown in Figure 9-4, emerged directly from PC technology. This interface was pioneered by PC spreadsheets and then carried over into PC databases. It preserves some aspects of formatted screens, adding a menu bar, pull-down menus, pop-up windows, and possibly mouse support.

The CUI is the first interface with sufficient horsepower to build object-action interfaces. To update an action-object system to support object-action, two ingredients are needed: (1) the ability easily to "select" display objects (that is, point at and express interest in these objects), and (2) the ability to pick from a rich set of actions that follow from the selection of objects. CUIs can do both of those.

The CUA name for the CUI is a mouthful: CUA Text Subset of the Graphical Model. The "Graphical Model" it refers to is described below; this is called the "Text Subset" because it can still run on a nongraphics display. The Text Subset Model is oriented towards character-mode PC applications and even aggressive dumb terminal applications.

Key issues for the Text Subset Model are:

- Object-action paradigm.
- Menu bars and pull-down menus.
- Pop-up windows and their behavior.

▼

### LEFT IN THE DUST

Both the CUA Entry Model and the CUA Text Subset Model are documented in the "CUA Basic Interface Design Guide" (BIDG). Anyone interested in building these interfaces should get very familiar with this manual because *that's all you're going to get*. IBM announced in June 1990 that, due to the rapid deployment of PCs (and, unspoken, to their desire to push customers toward the advanced interfaces), they would not be supplying tool support for either Entry or Text Subset levels.

Absent tools, there is only one method for building such user interfaces: Virtue. The user interface architecture must be implemented by a virtuous programmer who promises to follow the written documents conscientiously and exactly. Since programmer virtue is relatively low, this is an undependable method. In addition, development without tools is time-consuming, labor-intensive, and expensive.

The Entry Model and Text Subset will survive as useful guides for the many development shops building terminal-based applications, especially those utilizing CUA conventions like function key usage and screen layout. But most users, perhaps excepting software vendors who can amortize development costs over many sales, will find that, without tools, widespread application of these architectures is impractical.

## Graphical User Interface (CUA Graphical Model)

The graphical user interface (GUI, Figure 9-5) represents the state-of-the-practice for user interfaces. It adds graphics support, especially icons, to the CUI. Some people call this the WIMP interface: windows, icons, menus, pointers. GUIs turn up everywhere, from OS2/PM to Windows to Motif and beyond. (Many people believe that GUIs are the ultimate user interface. To their credit, CUA designers already recognize a further step, detailed below, that will improve on this one considerably.)

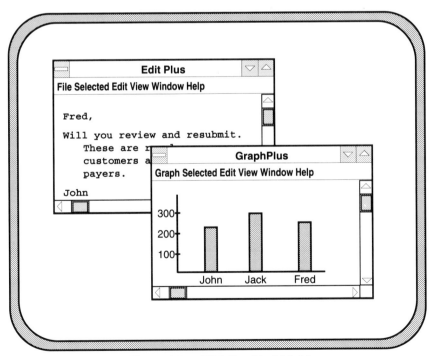

**Figure 9-5.** *CUA Graphical Model*

|                       | GUI                   | OOUI                          |
|-----------------------|-----------------------|-------------------------------|
| **Primary Entity**    | Application           | Object                        |
| **Visual Representative** | Window = Application | Icon = Object             |
| **Derivative Entity** | Icon = Shrunken Window | Window = One Viewer           |
| **Double-Click Means...** | "Run" an Application | "Open" a Viewer into an Object |

**Figure 9-6. Comparing semantics of the GUI with the OOUI.**

A GUI can multiplex applications on a single plate of glass so that a user can switch between, say, an Excel window and a Word window and even exchange some data between them. But each application remains discrete and monolithic within its own window. Although a GUI has the ability to deal with "objects" as described in the "Paradigm" section earlier in this chapter, it exploits these object concepts only "under the hood." The developer deals with the application-building componentry (windows, controls, scrollbars) as objects, but everything the user sees retains a traditional application structure. Contrast this GUI use of objects with the profound and thorough OOUI use of objects by referring to Figure 9-6.

CUA calls this interface the CUA Graphical Model. Key issues are:

- Window types.
- Controls (scrollbars, pushbuttons, radio buttons, etc.).
- Dialog boxes for communicating with the user.

### Object-Oriented User Interface (CUA Workplace Model)

The object-oriented user interface (OOUI, Figure 9-7) is the state-of-the-art user interface, replacing the GUI's application-oriented concepts with a universe of freely interacting objects. The OOUI invites users to

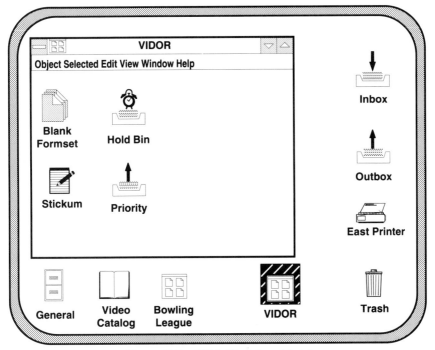

**Figure 9-7.** *CUA Workplace Model*

directly manipulate the objects on the glass and essentially build their own applications as they go. The OOUI simulates reality rather than just representing it.

When a kid playing the King's Quest computer game points at a coin on the ground, picks it up, and stores it in her pouch, this is OOUI behavior. (That sentence should perhaps read: ". . . 'points' at a 'coin' on the 'ground,' 'picks it up,' and 'stores' it in her 'pouch.' . . ." This is exactly the point; every noun and verb in an OOUI environment is a kind of metaphoric approximation of reality—or should that be 'real-ity'?) OOUIs also abound in "Draw" programs that, for example, let the user tug directly at shapes and stretch them out.

## AN OOUI DEMO

It is hard to appreciate the power of an OOUI workplace without encounter-ing one in action. Since such applications are still rare, we offer a short, verbal "demo" of a CUA Workplace Model application, with the caution that it is only a shadow of the real thing, for OOUIs are highly kinetic, responsive, and customizable.

An OOUI workplace (Figure 9-8) covers the whole plate of glass and comprises the user's universe. Populating this universe are a number of icons—the "objects" that give the OOUI its name.

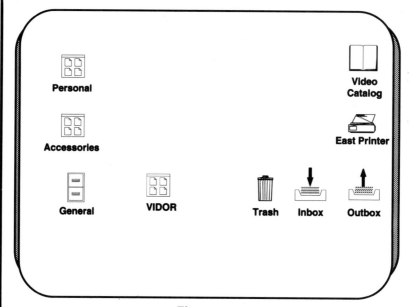

**Figure 9-8.**

A double mouse-click "opens" an object. In Figure 9-9, the inbox has been opened so that its contents are visible in a window. In an OOUI, a window is simply a *viewer* into an object, a kind of filter or magnifying glass that presents one way of looking at or into something. Notice that the window does not replace the primary object; the inbox icon is still there, highlighted to show that it is open.

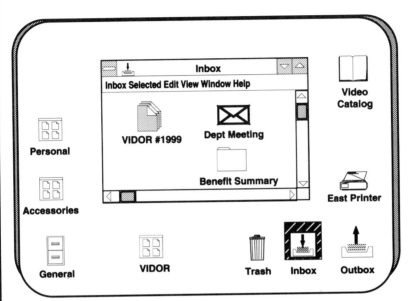

**Figure 9-9.**

In addition to opening objects and closing them back up, you can move them around the screen and drop them on top of other objects to activate various functions. For example, dropping a document onto the outbox will send the document; dropping it onto the printer will print it; dropping it onto the trash will toss it out. These are relatively simple interactions; you can push the metaphor further. For example, you can drop the printer onto the trash, thus removing the printer from the current desktop configuration, or you can drop the trash on the printer, thus printing the contents of the trash. The OOUI allows for many possibilities beyond the obvious.

This kind of direct manipulation works not only with an icon/object but also with any window/viewer of that object. The miniature icon on the left side of the title-bar in Figure 9-9 acts as a surrogate for the underlying icon/ object and can be moved about in exactly the same way. This is a convenience because windows often cover up their antecedent icon.

Although messy-desktop types might like hundreds of icons crowding and overlapping on their workplace, more organized people often make use of

**workareas** to group objects into manageable sets. A workarea is itself an object—a container, just like the inbox or the trash, except that it contains workplace objects. You can group objects into workareas any way you like—by task, icon color, object name, frequency or rarity of use, etc. To put an object into a workarea, you just drag it in. You can have any number of workareas open at the same time (they overlap and often hide one another completely). Workareas can contain other workareas.

Figure 9-10 shows the "Accessories" workarea opened up and viewed via a window. This workarea contains four objects, each of which can in turn be opened or drag-and-dropped.

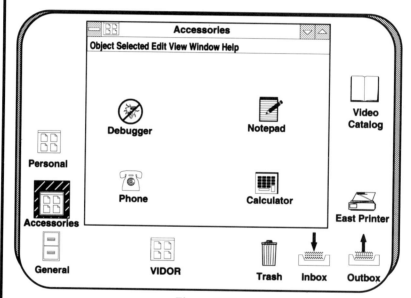

**Figure 9-10.**

Even the development environment plays by the same rules. Note the invaluable debugger icon. If you want to examine the internals of the work-area, opening this object will drop you into a debugger in the context of the host workarea. Or if you want to debug a particular object, you drop the debugger object onto it.

This interaction of icons to accomplish complicated, subtle, and possibly eccentric tasks, often completely unforeseen by the developer of the application, characterizes the OOUI workplace. There is no application to "run," just a variety of highly intelligent objects that the user can train, use, combine, and rearrange at will.

CUA calls the OOUI the CUA Workplace Model. All current CUA activity is aimed in this direction. Key issues for this model are:

- Object behavior.
- Drag-and-drop actions.
- Standard objects, containment, and views.

## GUIs vs. OOUIs

Most people confuse GUIs and OOUIs. Since the two use similar visual components, this is not surprising. But it is important to distinguish between them. Refer back to Figure 9-6. A GUI is a low-level UI abstraction, something like a "UI assembler." An OOUI utilizes GUI components as raw materials, but adds significant semantic content to the meaning of objects and user gestures. (The difference between them exactly parallels the difference between low-level file systems and high-level databases that have captured the semantics of the data.)

OOUIs, like most recent UI development, have been used primarily for textual applications. Later in the book, we look extensively at some exciting transaction-processing uses for OOUIs.

## Summary

OOUI technology brings us back around to an interface where users surround themselves with physical objects, learn how these objects behave, and freely set them to interacting. After years of computer-centric arrogance, the new technology has come to appreciate—and learned to incorporate—the deep knowledge embedded in older methods.

Designers of object-oriented user interfaces are often bemused to find themselves hanging out with employees who are near retirement. These are the people who can tell designers which forms used to be filled out in triplicate, who stamped what documents when, which file cabinets were locked, where the carbon copies went, where the pneumatic tubes ran, and what the color-coded labels meant. With their memories of the old manual methods, these old-timers are far more helpful in designing state-of-the-art computer systems than younger employees whose view of the organization has been distorted by years of typing obscure commands into dumb terminals.

# *10*

# *SAA into the Future*

One of SAA's leading architects has promised (some would say, *threatened*) that SAA will never be completed. He was not anticipating infinitely regressing development schedules, but rather making a commitment to continue applying standards and architecture to an ever-evolving information technology.

The pace of development that we have traced up until now will, if anything, accelerate in the future. As we write, there is work in progress throughout SAA. The radical points of change appear to be at the extreme poles of the architecture (Figure 10-1). We foresee substantive changes to the very bottom—the SAA software base—and to the very top in the Common Applications layer.

## Changes at the Bottom: Platform Restructuring

Despite all of the course corrections SAA has made in its brief history, some analysts believe that the most significant changes are yet to come. SAA as we know it may still be in a fairly primitive first phase. What we might call SAA Phase 1 has set out to provide consistency to user, programmer, and remote systems by hiding the underlying differences among the SAA platforms. These superficial "protective layers" provide good interoperability but poor portability characteristics. (Some design techniques discussed in Part IV, "Profiles," can dramatically increase portability characteristics even for SAA Phase 1 applications.)

SAA Phase 2 will have to take on a more fundamental and difficult task: actually changing the internals of the various SAA platforms so that they become truly more consistent with each other. Platform restructuring will solve consistency problems from within rather than masking them from without.

Is such an effort actually under way? Numerous published statements, plus presentations at open technical meetings such as GUIDE

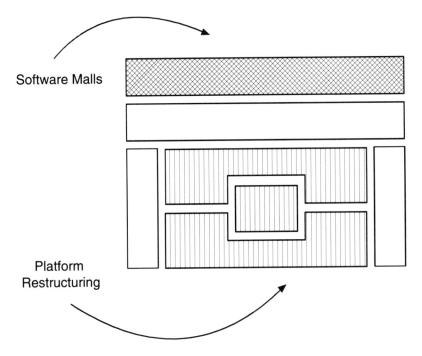

Software Malls

Platform
Restructuring

**Figure 10-1.** *SAA evolution at the bottom and the top*

and SHARE, have hinted at various aspects of this project. Expected
features of platform restructuring include the following:

- **SAA will become more open.** We have already noted that the standards and interfaces populating the SAA common layers are either
  open or published. Over time, other open standards will be added
  to the common layers and even to the SAA software base itself. As
  these standards become more integrated into SAA, SAA will start
  losing its identity as a vendor-supplied architecture and will
  become more like a framework for open standards.

- **SAA will become more interoperable.** IBM has announced that
  SAA will incorporate the major elements of the OSF/Distributed
  Computing Environment (DCE), a whole family of interfaces that
  govern interoperability among OSF participants. The OSF interfaces govern security, global naming services, remote procedure
  calls, distributed file systems, and others, providing the basic linkages for distributed systems. The alliance with OSF will give SAA
  systems strong interoperability with other SAA systems as well as
  OSF/DCE systems.

- **SAA will become more "structured."** Perhaps the most interesting initiative in SAA Phase 2 is a project that has shown up at SHARE "SAA Evolution" presentations as the "System Structure" project. This project puts all SAA ingredients—the various interfaces, plus the new open interfaces and services mentioned above, plus the OSF/DCE—under a coherent superframework. This framework then becomes a new system architecture with built-in support for handling distributed services and resources with integrated transactional integrity and system management.

The changes sketched here are so sweeping that you might ask whether this "restructuring" isn't really an entirely new architecture. That question will probably be decided on the basis of marketing considerations, not technical ones. This much is certain: the market is demanding multivendor solutions. SAA will have to deliver them, whether it enfolds these capabilities within itself or finds itself a place under the umbrella of a new, open superarchitecture.

## Changes at the Top: Software Malls

We have begun to suspect over the last few years that SAA describes not only an architecture for computer systems, but an architecture for commercial relationships as well. Recent developments have confirmed that SAA embodies IBM's new technology of business partnerships with other vendors.

AD/Cycle, described in Chapter 7, provides a good example. With its vast scope and its unprecedented hospitality to non-IBM software, AD/Cycle seems at first glance like a real anomaly. In fact, it is the first of a series of IBM-defined "composite applications"—huge frameworks for applications from many vendors that fit together to handle whole areas of business activity (Figure 10-2). Just as AD/Cycle assembles, orders, and interconnects software relating to application development, IBM's SystemView assembles software covering all phases of system management; Office Vision spans software for office activities; the Information Warehouse handles software related to accessing, managing, and analyzing data stored in heterogenous databases. CIM for manufacturing and the composite application called Insurance start extending the concept into specific industries. Each works the same way. IBM defines the overall job; divides it into categories of tasks; provides software to handle some of these tasks and recruits business partners to do the same; publishes a formal data model and implements it in a repository; and issues user-interface guidelines. Once the framework is established, products from various vendors can snap into place. Since all

| AD/Cycle | SystemView | Information Warehouse | OfficeVision |
|---|---|---|---|
| Cross-Life Cycle | Business Administration | Application & Decision Support | Address Book |
| Enterprise Modeling | Database Management | Data Delivery | Calendar |
| Analysis/Design | Host Management | Enterprise Data | Charts |
| Languages | Network Management | | Documents |
| Generators | Storage Management | | Inbasket/ Outbasket |
| Knowledge-Based Systems | | | Help/ Tutorial |
| Test/Maintain/ Reengineer | | | Reports |
| App Development Platform | | | Telephone |

**Figure 10-2.** *Composite applications: software malls*

participating applications must work together seamlessly, they have to interoperate, model their data consistently, and present an identical look-and-feel to the user. In other words, they must all subscribe to the same architecture. IBM has one ready: SAA.

We call these frameworks "software malls" because they do for computer software what your local "Northbrook Court" or "Serramonte Plaza" does for retailing. Each composite application brings together a variety of related products and services "under one roof." Customers enjoy one-stop shopping and the assurance that merchandise from different vendors will work together. IBM business partners, the "tenants" in the mall, get exposure, legitimacy, and lucrative comarketing opportunities. As the "mall developer," IBM sells the huge hardware systems that support these frameworks and gets many of the choicest software niches for itself.

As composite applications proliferate, it becomes clear that SAA's common interfaces, conventions, and protocols are valuable not in themselves, and not for some abstract good like "consistency," but because they provide the infrastructure for the software malls. The SAA architecture can be seen as a kind of structural shell—the foundation, the wiring, the design guidelines, and the facilities and services that all participants share. Once in place, it handles a number of "housekeeping" jobs and lets participants concentrate on improving and marketing their products.

The emergence of software malls clears up the mystery of what that odd Common Applications layer is doing at the top of the SAA diagram. And it tells us why SAA is called Systems Application Architecture instead of just Systems Architecture. Applications—huge, interlinked, multivendor mega-applications—are SAA's ultimate goal.

Or perhaps there is a goal even beyond that. To the extent that developers begin using these frameworks—to build their applications (AD/Cycle), manage their systems (SystemView), access information (Information Warehouse), etc.—they will find their applications further removed from, and less dependent on, the underlying SAA architecture. If, at some future time, the composite application itself is ported to another architecture (there is every indication, for example, that AD/Cycle is heading toward UNIX), the applications will go along for an essentially free ride. Thus, the business application, built atop the vendor application, that fits into the composite application, that rests atop SAA, gets a further boost toward multivendor portability.

### Toward Multivendor Solutions

Like any good troubleshooter, SAA's ultimate aim may be to put itself out of business. Both of the movements described here—platform restructuring and software malls—work toward satisfying the market's thirst for multivendor solutions. Platform restructuring attacks fundamental architectural inconsistency by implementing industry-architected interfaces in the very bowels of the SAA platforms. The software mall strategy defines structures for multivendor mega-applications that are so abstracted from platform considerations that they are becoming portable even from the architecture that spawned them. SAA as a distinct entity may blur to the point where it disappears.

Perhaps it is in the nature of software architecture to free its constituency from the perils of proprietorship. Certainly IBM's System Application Architecture, which was created to solve IBM internal development problems and help it compete with DEC, has ended up leading the way toward an open and distributed future.

# Part III

# Distributed Design Models

SAA is rich in components, but developers need more than components to get systems built. Cooperative processing raises complex structural issues—questions of component placement, interaction, and communication—and today's SAA does not provide much guidance. If SAA had been designed from the outset with distribution in mind, and if achieving flexible, cooperative processing applications were more clearly built into the foundations of SAA, the following chapters might not be necessary. As it is, however, designers have to supplement SAA (other system architectures share this problem) with large chunks of their own application architecture in order to get a framework that is complete enough to support real development work.

While every implementer is familiar with basic principles of system design, few are prepared for the supplemental design issues that crop up when a system is to be *distributed* among multiple platforms. Imagine a person whose one-man business has reached the point where he has to take on an associate. His organization becomes not just twice as complex, but perhaps eight times as complex. He has to worry not only about getting the work done, but about all sorts of additional issues around working together: how he and his associate will divide up the work; how they will divide up the profits; whether their relationship will be partner-to-partner or employee-to-boss; how they will share supplies and exchange information; whether they will meet in person, talk by phone, or write memos, and how often. All of these details have to be ironed out and continuously tended to. Distribution brings just these sorts of additional design complications to computer systems.

The complexities do not stop there. Breaking an application into pieces for cooperative processing purposes becomes even more challenging when the application in question involves **transactions**. Transactions are complex packages of work that must be kept coordinated and synchronized at all times. Keep in mind that any transaction processing system—which is what most cooperative processing applications are—places extra burdens on the design models discussed here. We discuss transactions, and how to distribute them, in detail in Chapter 12.

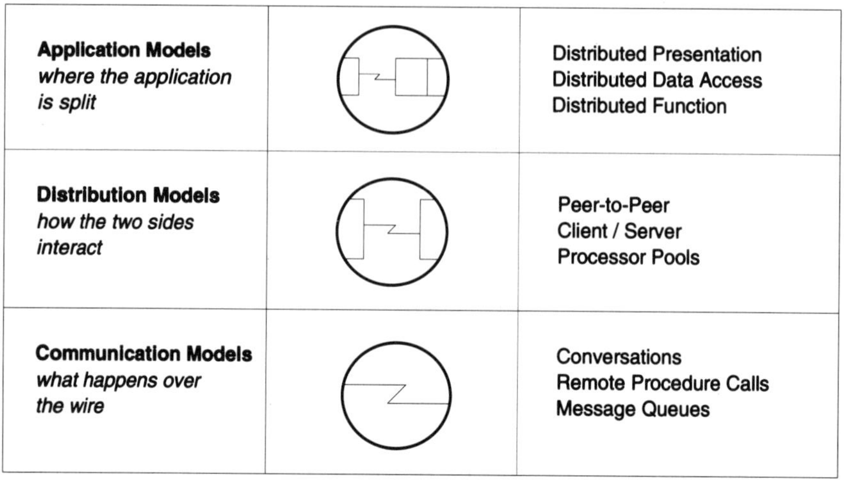

| Application Models *where the application is split* | | Distributed Presentation Distributed Data Access Distributed Function |
| --- | --- | --- |
| Distribution Models *how the two sides interact* | | Peer-to-Peer Client / Server Processor Pools |
| Communication Models *what happens over the wire* | | Conversations Remote Procedure Calls Message Queues |

**Figure III-1.**   *Distributed design at three levels of magnification*

## Three Design Issues

As you start arranging components end-to-end to achieve a working system, you confront three general design issues:

- First, where can the application be split?
- Then, how do the two sides interact across the split?
- Finally, what happens over the wire that connects them?

As you might expect, there are a number of places that an application can be split, a number of ways the sides can interact, and a number of ways for them to communicate. Figure III-1 divides the design process into the three categories—application, distribution, and communication—and lists the alternative models for each. In a sense, each stripe of the chart represents a closer-in view of the distribution. Application models lay out where the split occurs in relation to the whole system. Distribution models move in to isolate the interaction between the parties on either side of the split. Communication models zoom in tight to examine the link between the sides, independent of what is communicating with what.

In none of the categories are the models mutually exclusive. You do not have to settle on just one of the alternatives; in fact, you should avoid that. A robust cooperative processing system may use all three application models, all three distribution models, and eventually all three communication models many times over, sometimes simultaneously. Understand them all so that you can decide which is best suited to which strand of the complex system you will be designing.

# 11

# *Application Models*

If you are going to take an application that once ran on a single platform and split it up to run on multiple platforms, the first question is obvious: Where shall it be split?

Consider this question in terms of a familiar model. Figure 11-2 represents the way people have thought about information systems for years. At the back is some magnetic or optical surface that stores raw data, and a layer of data access software that delivers data to the application. At the front is some form of display and a layer of presentation software to render the application activity for the display. At the center is the application function—usually business logic—where the real work of the application gets done.

Until recently most systems were monolithic, with the three pieces running in the same place. Turning such a monolithic, **local processing** system into a distributed one means breaking into it somewhere, at a point we'll call a **split**, moving the split-off portion to another machine, and building a communications link between.

The following three application models suggest various places that the system can be divided and the effects of each kind of split. Distributed Presentation splits off the presentation piece; Distributed Data Access splits off the data access piece; Distributed Function actually splits the application logic somewhere in the middle.

Within these three general families of application models, there are countless points at which the actual split can occur. Developers of cooperative processing systems tend to exploit a few over and over. Some of these splits are "architected" and others are not. An architected split is

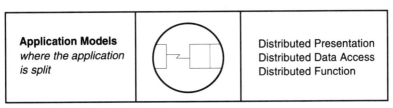

**Figure 11-1.** *Distributed application models*

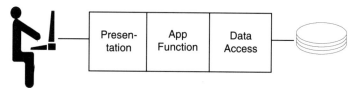

**Figure 11-2.** *Cross section of an information system*

one that SAA (in our case) officially recognizes with an interface. Non-architected splits are those that developers may have found useful, and for which there may even be product support, but which do not have an officially sanctioned interface.

## Distributed Presentation

One popular application model is Distributed Presentation. It involves splitting off the presentation piece and relocating part or all of its functionality to the workstation. This dramatically changes what the presentation can look like and do because workstations have wonderful capabilities in the user interface area. Three main Distributed Presentation splits are shown in Figure 11-3.

### Distributed Display

SAA support has focused on one particular style of Distributed Presentation called Distributed Display, familiarly known by the evocative name "screen-scraper." A screen-scraper breaks off the presentation block at a low level, very close to the display device. It intercepts the

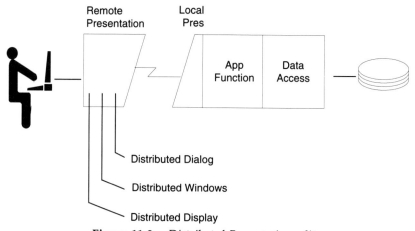

**Figure 11-3.** *Distributed Presentation splits*

terminal-bound data stream and transforms it into a snazzy, colorized workstation-user interface, all unbeknownst to the back end. The value of screen-scrapers for large host-based systems is obvious. You can leave the bulk of the application on the mainframe and give it a significantly higher value user interface with some fairly quick and easy new front-end programming. (Screen-scraping does bring along certain longer term development and maintenance headaches, which we explore in Chapter 15.)

### Distributed Windows

Another form of Distributed Presentation, widely used and architected in the UNIX community but not currently architected within SAA, might be called Distributed Windows. It breaks off an entire windowing system—including windows, icons, menus, and pointers—and places it on the workstation. The premier example of this split is the UNIX X Windows system. X Windows provides a very smart dumb terminal called an "X server," which supports a mouse and a full windowing system. The X server can be remote-controlled by an "X client" application running elsewhere on the network. (In stand-alone environments, X server and X client can be two processes on the same machine.) Here, unlike Distributed Display, the application program on the back end needs to be written explicitly for the distributed windowing environment.

### Distributed Dialog

Distributed Dialog involves a still higher-level split within the Distributed Presentation model. You move whole portions of an application's user interface to the front end by downloading specifications for business forms or transactions (including field editing and processing rules) and then invoke these specifications to execute when needed. DEC supports a product called DECforms that takes this approach. SAA has no architected interface for Distributed Dialog, but SAA developers still resort to this technique often. In Chapter 19, we look at a multifaceted implementation profile called a formset that can be configured to run as a Distributed Dialog.

### Shared Characteristics

No matter which of these specific splits you exploit, the general characteristics of Distributed Presentation are the same. They are:

- The application itself—the very center of control—remains on the back-end machine. To one degree or another, presentation chores are off-loaded to the workstation, but there is no question as to which machine dominates.

- Distributed Presentation is useful for migrating existing host software to cooperative processing. The majority of the application code (*all* of it in the case of screen-scrapers) remains where it was.

- Even when more powerful application models are available, certain situations will still call for Distributed Presentation: host-controlled dialogs (log-on or security questionnaires), infrequently used or unexpected dialogs, or interfaces into systems over which you have no control.

▼

## HIGH-LEVEL AND LOW-LEVEL SPLITS

This first application model has introduced the notion of low- and high-level splits. Since low and high are arbitrary designations, in programming as in outer space, some explanation is necessary.

Most programmers know these terms in relation to programming languages. Low-level languages are closer to the vocabulary of the device than to the vocabulary of the application: an assembler language is low-level because, for example, its MOVE and TEST verbs relate directly to the operation of the computer. High-level languages, by contrast, deal instead with application-style verbs such as COMPUTE or UPDATE.

Similarly, a low-level interface uses a vocabulary close to the language of the device. The Distributed Display interface consists of the terminal's own codes, so it is extremely low-level. For Distributed Windows, the verbs on the wire are at the level of CreateWindow or WatchMouse—not exactly the vocabulary of an accounting application, but certainly the vocabulary of a layer where the system controls the presentation. Way up in Distributed Dialog you find verbs like GetAuditForm—recognizable application terminology.

In Distributed Presentation, as Figure 11-4 shows, higher-level splits are toward the back end, that is, toward the application. But, in the Distributed Data Access application model below, directions are reversed. Higher-level interfaces are toward the front end, because the application logic which owns the vocabulary of the application is in the *middle*. Remember that "high-level" means close to the application—in this case, toward the center. "Low-level" means near the devices, and that means toward each edge.

High and low are not value judgments. Low-level splits tend to require more computerese but they are also more general. High-level splits tend to be clearer to the user's purpose but much more specialized. The important consideration is which interface best suits the job at hand.

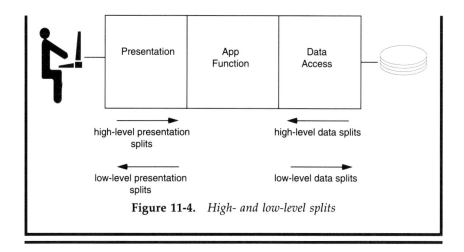

**Figure 11-4.**  *High- and low-level splits*

## Distributed Data Access

The opposite of the Distributed Presentation model is Distributed Data Access. Here you split off the data access function, move it to a machine further back in the system, and keep the bulk of the application on the workstation or LAN server. Distributed Data Access is a well-known and widely used technique. Both of its main split points (Figure 11-5) are architected in SAA.

### Distributed Files

The lower-level Distributed File interface provides one useful model. This interface splits along the boundary between application and file system, allowing a program's files to exist elsewhere on the network.

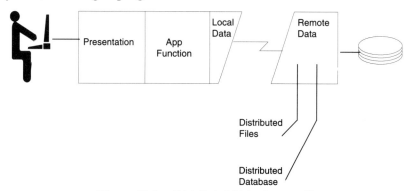

**Figure 11-5.**  *Distributed Data Access splits*

Distributed File verbs include Open, Close, Read, Write, and Position. Distributed Files are widely implemented on LANs. SAA architects this interface and calls it Distributed Data Management (DDM). Other popular Distributed File systems are the Sun Network File System (NFS) and the OSF/DCE Andrew File System (AFS).

### Distributed Database

Much more popular is the high-level Distributed Database interface. This split takes advantage of the cleavage between the application and the database management system right at the point where the SQL statement is invoked. It probably represents the single most successful split in distributed computing, but, as we will see in Chapter 13, it has its own domain of use and misuse. The trade press hypes this split under the name "client/server computing." This is unfortunate since "client/server" is a useful architectural term in its own right, wholly independent of database issues.

### Shared Characteristics

Both Distributed Data Access application models share these characteristics:

- Virtually all cooperative processing applications have some use for Distributed Data Access.
- This is the simplest of all the application models to use. The developer does not even have to know whether the application is distributed or not.
- Despite its ease of use, Distributed Data Access can leave developers responsible for some data-sharing and integrity problems.
- Empirical evidence shows that the application-database seam is an extremely busy and potentially expensive one. Using it as an all-purpose distribution point can drive up costs astronomically.

## Distributed Function

For maximum application flexibility, the model of choice is Distributed Function, shown in Figure 11-6. Here the split occurs somewhere within the application logic, and the function itself gets divided up among platforms. These separated function blocks then communicate by sending each other messages. As a result, distributed function systems are

**Figure 11-6.** *Distributed Function*

also called **message-based systems.** This application model allows the developer total control over what function gets placed where, enabling him to finely tune the performance, trust, and integrity of the system.

Predictably, Distributed Function applications are harder to build than other application models. For one thing, in many cooperative processing systems the platform on one side of the split is of a different type from the platform on the other side. Many first-generation cooperative processing applications were written in C on the workstation side and COBOL on the host side; so when function gets distributed in this environment, half of the application logic will have to be written in one language and half in the other. Not only does this require double skillsets and most likely two different teams, but design problems abound. A designer has to decide early on where a function will run and then assign it to one development team or the other. If later, after some prototyping, he decides that the function would do better on the other side, it needs to be *converted*, not just moved.

An even deeper problem looms. The cleavage points do not fall at fixed locations, like those in the Distributed Data Access application model, but come instead along interapplication "grooves" built by the programmer. Many older systems, written for monolithic uses, are not grooved at all. These have to be rewritten before they can be split up. Even systems built using modular programming techniques are often hard to split because the module boundaries were designed for a different purpose. In Chapter 14, we recommend techniques based on object-oriented concepts that you can use to build permanent grooves into new applications.

Distributed Function has these characteristics:

- It allows for the ultimate in flexible function and data placement, which is the cornerstone of performance-tuning in cooperative processing.
- Existing systems do not migrate well to Distributed Function. Unless you have been putting grooves in your existing applications, you will have to do a major overhaul before they can support this split.

• With the appropriate "paradigm shift," Distributed Function applications can become easy to build. You will have to change how you and your team think about structuring applications.

▼

## THOU SHALT KNOW THEM BY THEIR MESSAGES

Notice that the splits match the messages that travel across them. A certain kind of split generates a certain kind of message, and a certain kind of message implies a certain kind of split. A designer can start at either point.

A designer usually thinks about where she wants to split a system and then figures out suitable messages. Alternatively, she could design a message protocol for a component and then see what kind of split it requires. Figure 11-7 shows hypothetical examples of messages that come along with various application models.

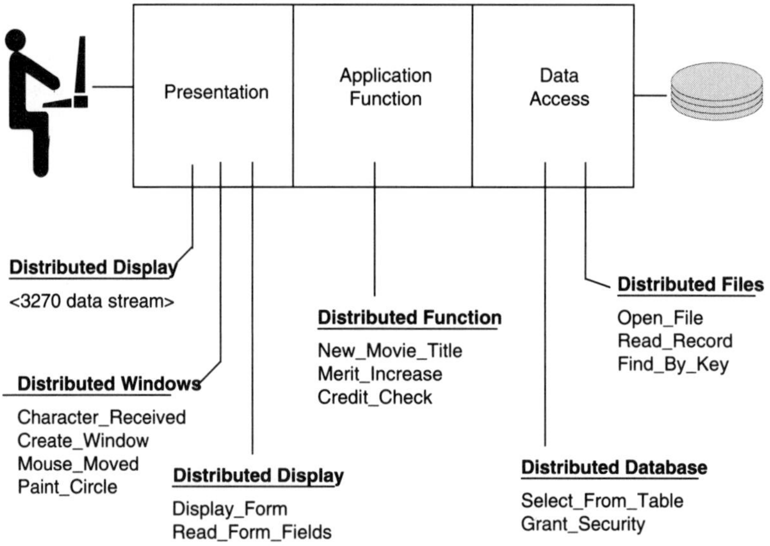

| Presentation | Application Function | Data Access |
|---|---|---|

**Distributed Display**

<3270 data stream>

**Distributed Windows**

Character_Received
Create_Window
Mouse_Moved
Paint_Circle

**Distributed Display**

Display_Form
Read_Form_Fields

**Distributed Function**

New_Movie_Title
Merit_Increase
Credit_Check

**Distributed Files**

Open_File
Read_Record
Find_By_Key

**Distributed Database**

Select_From_Table
Grant_Security

**Figure 11-7.** *Sample messages across a distributed application*

## Which Application Model to Use?

Be ready to use all of these application models. Most cooperative processing applications worth the name will have strands where the presentation gets distributed, strands where the data access gets distributed, and many strands where the function is distributed. Each model is ideal for certain jobs and highly inefficient for others. A developer should have all three in his repertoire.

Which model you start with depends on your current situation. If you are sitting on a large mainframe-based system, you will tend to start by distributing and upgrading the presentation piece. This is a good short-term tactic, but not a long-term strategy. Strategic new development tends to start with a fundamental rethinking of how to handle data access and how to structure the application for distributed function. With an architected master plan in hand, you will be able to coordinate these efforts so that short-term tactical solutions generate system components that will remain useful when newer strategic solutions arrive.

# *12*

# *Distribution Models*

Quite independent of *where* the application is split for distribution is the matter of *how* the distribution works. What are the dynamics of the split? How do the two sides—whether split in presentation, data, or function—relate to one another? Distribution models address these issues.

The processors involved in a distributed system can relate to one another as peers, as client and server, or as members of a pool of processors. All these roles are precisely defined and well documented in the technical literature.

### Peer-to-Peer

In a peer-to-peer relationship, the two distributed processes relate as architectural equals, as Figure 12-2 shows. Either process can start a conversation with the other; either can send or receive messages according the script laid out by the developer; either can terminate the conversation after carrying out a piece of business.

Since distribution occurs frequently in the real world, a noncomputer analogy can clarify each distribution model. Imagine that a person starts a business making custom glassware. For the longest time possible, she does all the work herself: producing the products, handling the sales, doing the accounting, wrapping, and shipping. As the business prospers, she hires employees and starts distributing the activity in her business. Soon there is a glassblowing department, a sales department, an accounting department, and a shipping department. These four

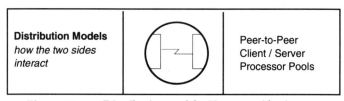

**Figure 12-1.** *Distribution models: How two sides interact*

**Figure 12-2.** *Peer-to-peer distribution*

departments relate on a peer-to-peer basis. The salesperson passes orders to the glassblower. The glassblower passes product to the shipping department. The shipping department sends paperwork to accounting. Periodically, sales might shout to the glassblower to work faster because orders are piling up. (The glassblower's reply might be nonarchitected.) Any department can initiate conversations in any order with any other department. These conversations can be formal request-response, or they might be a broadcast on the PA system ("Listen, everybody: Friday we close early").

In computer systems, too, peer-to-peer models allow parties to communicate freely. Peer-to-peer interactions are extremely flexible. They work especially well for unexpected activity from any peer or for activity in the reverse direction from the usual. However, in more predictable situations, peer-to-peer may provide more generality than anybody needs, or wants.

The need to accommodate an almost infinite variety of interactions makes peer-to-peer systems harder to build than some other distribution models. To make matters worse, traditional programming languages, built as they are around the notion of subordinate modules (subroutines), have trouble expressing the notion of peer modules (so-called coroutines). Object-orientation, as we will see in Chapter 14, provides more possibilities for modules in either role and will make richer peer-to-peer implementations easier in the future.

You can see a good example of a true peer-to-peer interaction in the set of processes we will call a Replica Manager. A workstation may need to store a replica of a frequently updated host table—bond prices, for example. When the system starts up, the workstation asks the host for the current table and receives it—a simple request-reply interaction. As bond prices change during the day, the host broadcasts these new figures to all interested workstations. Either party can initiate any sort of interaction at any time.

## Client/Server

In client/server interactions (Figure 12-3), one process (the client) makes requests of another process (the server), which performs some service and sends a reply.

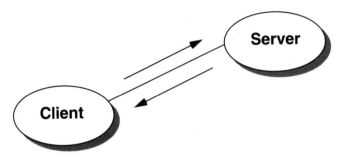

**Figure 12-3.**   *Client/server distribution*

Our glass company periodically uses client/server architecture when tax time rolls around. It hires a CPA, its tax "server," to make the calculations and fill out the forms. The CPA doesn't necessarily know anything about the glass business, just as she knows little about the details of the thirty-nine other clients she works for. Her job is to perform a fairly standard service and return the results.

Where peer-to-peer is generalized, client/server is specialized and constrained to a certain type of interaction. Consequently a much simpler, prewired communication protocol can be used, and the programmer's job is much easier.

The hierarchic nature of client/server builds a "bias" into the role of each process (client will ask, server will respond). This bias simplifies the programming job considerably, but there is a downside. Hierarchic systems are like rivers with strong currents. As long as the developer goes with the flow (client requesting, server replying), he gets to his destination fast. But fighting the current is difficult. If the application even *occasionally* requires the server to turn around and request something of the client (as in the Replica Manager above), the developer faces a tough swim.

Fortunately, the vast majority of distributed interactions in a cooperative processing system are pure request-reply protocols and can achieve their objectives with client/server architecture. But you should be familiar with other distribution models and be ready to turn to them when appropriate.

Keeping client/server in perspective is difficult in the face of a recent wave of ill-considered boosterism. To our great discomfort, many vendors and writers have redefined this useful term to describe a specific system layout—namely, "client" workstations, usually on LANs, talking to a (usually database) "server" on a host machine. While this is a good example of client/server distribution, it is by no means the only one.

There are many kinds of clients and servers. Look, for example, at the UNIX product X Windows discussed in the last chapter. The application code running on some multiuser machines is the "X client" and the workstation/terminal is the "X server"; in this case, the client lives on the big machine, and the small terminal acts as its display server. Another example: a dedicated hardware clock could be a time server on a network, with clients ranging from mainframes to Macintoshes. Or a mainframe client process could invoke an Actuary-Server that runs on a supermini. In UNIX, we quite frequently see a client application on the host accessing a downstream X server on a workstation and an upstream database server running on a mainframe.

It should be clear that the client is not always a workstation and the server is not always a database server. The client is not always on the small machine, and the server is not always the big machine. Client/server describes relationships between processes, not platforms.

▼

## DIFFERENT SERVER CLASSES ENRICH CLIENT/SERVER MODEL

Servers generally fall into one of four classes, listed below beginning with low-level servers and ending with high-level servers. As a general rule, the higher the level of the server, the more leverage is gained across the distributed link. But all have an important role to play in cooperative and distributed systems.

The **device server** supplies basic device services to clients, allowing these clients to share expensive devices (a laser printer) or to access a shared resource (a centralized clock for synchronized time stamps).

The **file server** shares files among a community of clients in a way that offers more protection and integrity than a mere disk server (a type of device server) would. This is a form of the Distributed Data Access application model.

The **database server** shares logical databases with its clients. (This is the server that people usually mean when they refer to "client/server.") The message format is invariably some type of SQL. The server processes the SQL and returns an "answer set" to the client. Database servers implement the Distributed Data Access application model.

The **transaction server** performs transactions for clients. The client can call a transaction (e.g., NewHire or ChangeOrder), which executes on the server, typically accessing the server's database. A transaction server implements the Distributed Function application model.

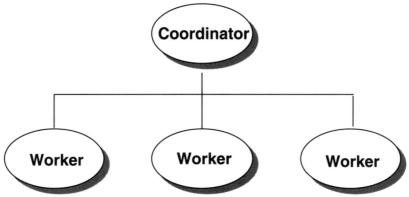

**Figure 12-4.** *Processor pool distribution*

The advantage of client/server distribution lies in its simplicity, not its power. In fact, client/server is the least powerful of the distribution models. Peer-to-peer offers far greater architectural generality. Both peer-to-peer and processor pools (discussed next) exploit parallel processing far better. But, for the next few years, while distributed systems remain so difficult to build, simplicity will be prized above all other virtues, and client/server architecture will remain at the forefront of computing technology.

## Processor Pools

The processor-pools model (Figure 12-4) calls for a **coordinator** process to break a large computing problem into small pieces, parcel them out among an army of essentially interchangeable **workers** (on different CPUs), gather the results back in, and collate a final result. Processor pools show up far less in I/S than in scientific applications. This type of distribution works for large, compute-intensive programs that can be easily segmented, such as weather forecasting, matrix manipulation, and image enhancement.

The glass company might decide to branch out into chandeliers that have hundreds of small components. A manager could farm out the jobs of making these components to various independent glassblowers. They deliver their pieces back to the company, and the manager does the final assembly.

Clearly, processor pools can bring enormous raw horsepower to applications where the problem is segmentable. So far, success in general commercial applications has been limited, though processor pools are beginning to show up in parallel database machines and distributed expert systems. Advanced research projects have experimented with using massively parallel environments for distributed transaction processing. Although commercial processor-pool architectures will be hard to build (their principle feature is decidedly *not* simplicity), they will absolutely demolish other approaches in terms of performance.

---

## FIVE ROLES IN THREE MODELS

When it comes to distribution, a process can assume any of five roles, or even several roles at the same time. It can relate to multiple counterparts as a peer, client, server, coordinator, or worker. For example, a process on a host computer might be a claim-processing *server* to a workstation client. When it needs some policy information, it becomes a *client* to a database server. And occasionally it will be a *peer* to a process, acting as *coordinator* to a processor pool where a bunch of *workers* are calculating mortality figures.

Fluid roles in multiple relationships also characterize human interactions. Any individual can be simultaneously a parent, child, boss, and subordinate. To think that a person—or a process or platform—permanently plays just one role regardless of the circumstances (as some "client/server computing" partisans advocate) flies in the face of everything we know about human and computer sociology.

---

## Transactions: Distributed and Otherwise

In laying out various models for the way that distributed processes can interact, we have until now factored out the added complexity that comes from working with transactions. Nearly all cooperative processing systems process transactions, and they do have to take the requirements of transaction processing into account.

A transaction, also called a unit-of-work, is a piece of business logic that either executes in its entirety, updating all of the resources that it touches, or else aborts entirely, leaving all resources unchanged. This quality of transactional wholeness is called "integrity." Most commonly, the resource that a transaction works against is a database. However, sophisticated transaction processing environments may involve many resources: multiple databases, files, and in-memory

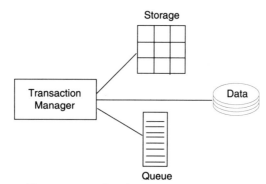

**Figure 12-5.** *Local transaction management*

storage or queues. Every one of these resources must be either fully updated on a commit or fully backed out on a rollback.

This daunting task has been made manageable by commercial **transaction-management** software such as SAA's CICS, IMS/TM, or the base OS/400 operating system transactional components. All of these transaction managers were originally built to accommodate only "local transactions," where all affected resources are located on the same machine as the transaction manager (Figure 12-5).

A more complex transaction processing configuration is a "remote transaction" (Figure 12-6). In this case, a transaction initiated by one transaction manager crosses a robust communication link and updates resources on a remote environment. We see this frequently when client workstations update data on a database server.

While remote transaction involves only a single remote environment, true "distributed transaction" processing updates resources in multiple remote environments. It is considerably more difficult to handle than either local or remote transactions. In this configuration (Figure 12-7), far-flung resources need to be committed or rolled back with network-wide integrity. Possible failure scenarios multiply: one or more of these systems could fail; one or more of the communication links between them could go down.

Managing this extremely demanding task requires a technique called "two-phase commit." The two-phase commit process allows for network resources to be alerted to the impending update (phase 1), then committed all at once with a networkwide signal (phase 2). Two-phase

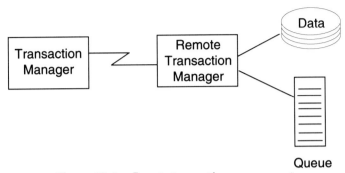

**Figure 12-6.** *Remote transaction management*

commit has implications for the communication link as well as for the software at each end.

Implementation details lie beyond the scope of this book and beyond the scope of most application developers. Two-phase commit capabilities should be provided by system software vendors as part of their database and transaction-management infrastructure. Until it is, developers should try to avoid situations where two-phase commit is necessary.

Avoiding the two-phase commit is usually possible. Most distributed applications will not need distributed transaction processing and can depend on one of the simpler transaction-processing configurations instead. For example, a Distributed-Presentation or Distributed-Function front end can cause a host-based local transaction to execute. Alternatively, a LAN server with a transaction manager can route remote transactions to a host transaction manager for processing.

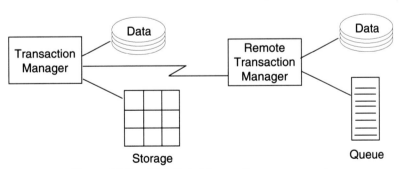

**Figure 12-7.** *Distributed transaction management*

Still, a developer should understand and recognize all three levels of transaction management. If you find that you need a highly sophisticated remote or distributed environment, look to your architecture for a solution, buy a third-party solution, or come up with a simpler application alternative.

# *13*

# *Communication Models*

Finally, we move in close to take a look at the innermost part of a design—the machinery that ties the sides together. Communication models describe various delivery vehicles for the bigger-picture distribution models and application models.

If you notice a similarity to Chapter 12's distribution models and begin to suspect that our communication models are just new names for old relationships, remember that the emphasis here is on the *mechanics* of how the relationships are implemented. The distinction between distribution models and communication models is the same as that between database systems and file systems. Both database systems and file systems have something to do with accessing and updating data, but database systems take the point of view of the data model, while file systems look at which file access verbs accomplish the same logical action.

SAA architects are in the process of defining three communication models (conversations, remote procedure calls, and message queues), though most current implementations exploit only the first of the three.

## Conversations

When all parties in a particular communication sequence cooperate to create an interaction, this is called a conversation. Conversations are the communication model implemented in the LU6.2 protocol and presented to the developer as the SAA Communications Interface.

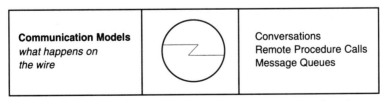

| Communication Models<br>*what happens on*<br>*the wire* | | Conversations<br>Remote Procedure Calls<br>Message Queues |
|---|---|---|

**Figure 13-1.** *Communication models: What happens on the wire*

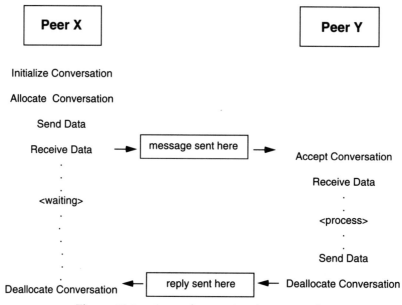

**Figure 13-2.** *A sample request-reply conversation*

To understand conversations, imagine two people communicating by talking and listening through a hose. Note first that it is not possible for either of them to talk and listen at the same time. Note second that, to make clear communication possible under these circumstances, they have to set up certain ground rules, called collectively a "protocol," that govern their interaction. Perhaps they will agree to take turns talking and listening; then they also have to agree who will start, otherwise they might both talk at once or both sit there listening. In another scenario, they might agree that one person will be the command-giver and the other person will only give back acknowledgements ("Got it," or "How's that again?"), as illustrated in Figure 13-2. Or perhaps one will only speak and the other will only listen. There are many possible protocols, expanded geometrically by the fact that there may be ten hoses going to ten confederates. (One common protocol: All ten of you listen to this, and the first with the answer yell back down the hose.)

The conversational model's greatest strength and greatest weakness is its generality. You can do anything with it, but you have to lay out precisely what you plan to do. This model is ideal for implementing peer-to-peer distribution models, but it is flexible enough to be pressed into service for constructing client/server or processor-pool interactions as well.

In practice, most development shops do not leave it to the application programmer to implement conversational communications. Since a small number of standard conversations will handle nearly all of your interactions, you can have a communication specialist package up these few for you and give them to the application programmer to invoke as "Request-from-Accounting-Database" or "Credit-Check."

Conversations can, in theory, be transactional or nontransactional, but not all conversational implementations support the transaction option. To exploit transactional conversations, the SAA Communications Interface needs to be supplemented with the SAA Resource Recovery Interface. In SAA environments where RRI is not yet supported, you may need to use the underlying LU6.2 communications product (usually named Advanced Program-to-Program Communication, or APPC).

## Remote Procedure Calls

The remote procedure call (RPC) is coming into wider use because it handles much of the day-to-day work of distributed systems very simply. RPC (Figure 13-3) is exactly what its name suggests: a procedure call to some remote subroutine. It works so well because it exploits cleavages that already exist in software.

Ever since the "structured" revolution of the early seventies, programmers have tended to break large systems up into hierarchies of modules that can be CALLed as needed: an inventory system may CALL a parts lookup subroutine that in turn CALLs an indexed search subroutine. This kind of structured, modular programming has simplified complex systems and facilitated breaking a large development chore into more manageable chunks. RPC products enlist those same built-in CALL statements to perform another valuable service. Without further changes to the source code (in some of the products, at least), the CALL statement will create and route a message to a separate machine, execute the subroutine, return results to the CALLing program, and continue execution.

At first glance, an RPC might look like just a particular type of conversational protocol—a request-reply conversation. In fact, some simpler RPCs have been built in just this way. But RPC technology has advanced at an enormous rate, and a number of features that go well beyond conversational implementations are now becoming standard. For example, automatic data conversion between differing machine architectures is almost universal. Directory services make it possible to put the machine and task location of the CALLed service in a table so that a client does not need to know where the service provider lives.

**Client Computer**                    **Server Computer**

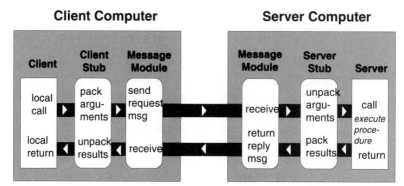

**Figure 13-3.**  *Structure of a remote procedure call*

Authentication algorithms can be built into the RPC to let a mutually suspicious client and server verify the other party's identity.

Other imminent features will support richer control structures than simple request-reply. Coming up is asynchronous RPC, where a caller may wish to invoke a remote service to start a long-running task and be notified only when a result is obtained. Another is a "callback" capability that allows the CALLed service to RPC back in the reverse direction if it needs some special attention.

Another area of innovation is the "transactional RPC." In transaction processing, a whole series of calls may be issued against multiple resource managers. Transactional integrity depends on all of these resources, regardless of location, being either committed or completely rolled back when the unit-of-work is completed. The transactional RPC will ultimately revolutionize transaction-processing applications, but industrial-strength versions will be a long time coming in the environments where they are most needed. For now, developers must read the fine print and understand exactly what a given RPC can do and what it can't.

SAA will be adopting the RPC that has been defined by the Open Software Foundation as part of its DCE. These SAA RPCs are still in the future, but a number of third-party products are available today.

### Message Queuing

The least developed of SAA's communication models is message queuing (Figure 13-4). Since 1989, IBM presentations at SHARE have alluded to this approach and promised a developer interface, probably in the form of a new CPI element, that would address this model.

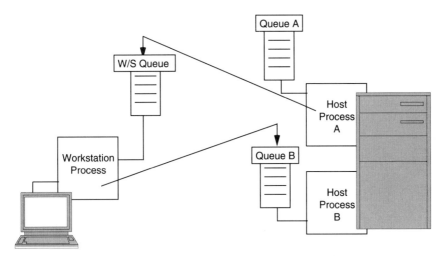

**Figure 13-4.** *Message queuing communicates via distributed queuing*

The message queuing model is intended for high-volume, networked transaction-processing applications. Here transaction queues are scattered around a distributed environment. A process can open and close a queue or get and leave queue messages. Message traffic is said to be "connectionless." This doesn't mean there are no wires; it means that there are no fixed "sessions"—connections between two points that extend over a number of transmissions. One way to think about message queuing, if you are familiar with IMS, is that it is a networked IMS/TM. Assuming a robust implementation with sufficient performance, this is a powerful paradigm for ATM networks or reservation systems that need to deal with large volumes of asynchronous activity.

## Fitting Models Together

We have now looked at three levels of design models—models for the application split, for distribution of resources, and for communication among platforms. In various combinations, they offer a vast range of possible system designs.

As we said at the beginning of this section and can't repeat too often, *use all of them* in their appropriate places. Remember this even in the face of pressure from vendors—a vendor whose product implements one of these models will tend to view the whole world that way. For example, several vendors of distributed database products (application model: Distributed Data Access; distribution model: client/server;

communication model: RPC) market their wares under the term "client/server computing." If you let them sell you this arrangement as your platform, you will restrict your design options to this one model only. By all means, use Distributed Database as a *component,* just not as a *platform.* Developing a religious devotion to one model or another will limit your choices and compromise your system design.

In theory, you can mix and match from any of these layers. In practice, you probably won't want to. Certain combinations work beautifully, and others don't make much sense. Some models that are meaningful together are:

Distributed databases:
    Distributed Data Access
    Client/server
    RPC

X-Windows:
    Distributed Presentation
    Client/server
    RPC

Peer applications:
    Distributed Function
    Peer-to-peer
    Conversations

Remote application services:
    Distributed Function
    Client/server
    RPC

Distributed transaction queuing:
    Distributed Function
    Peer-to-peer
    Message queuing

Parallel database machines:
    Local
    Processor pool
    Conversations

## Cooperative Processing vs. Client/Server

The previous few chapters lay out an entire taxonomy of Distributed Computing. In this context, the pervasive and somewhat engineered confusion about the relationship between cooperative processing and client/server seems easily resolved. They are not the same thing. They are not competitive alternatives. To say that cooperative processing means front-ending your mainframe whereas client/server means downsizing to LANs seriously distorts two useful terms. To claim that cooperative processing is the old and difficult way and that client/server is the new, easy, and economical way does a long-term disservice to vendors and users alike.

"Cooperative processing" designates any distributed system that has a user interface machine on front and presents a single-system image to the user. This includes front-ending mainframes, LAN-based distributed databases, and enough other configurations to fill a book, namely this one.

"Client/server," properly used, refers not to LAN-based platforms, but to the architectural setup whereby processes relate hierarchically. It is an important component in building a cooperative processing or any distributed processing system. You no more have to choose between cooperative processing and client/server than you do between subroutines and IF statements. They are not on the same level, they do not do the same thing, and they are not in competition.

What has been called "client/server computing" has gained so many partisans because it promises economy, flexibility, and a kind of grassroots sociology that many people find appealing. We believe that all this, and more, can be gained within the overall context of the much more durable system design called cooperative processing.

# 14

## Distributed Design and Objects

Of all the supplemental design concepts necessary for building distributed transaction-based systems, the one that really turns the corner for designers is the notion of object-orientation. OO, a hot concept in some circles and virtually unknown in others, provides a radically new point of view on system design—one where the familiar system building blocks, "data" and "code," get replaced by new entities called "objects" and "messages." OO seems to be part of the massive technological/conceptual upheaval that has led to cooperative processing. In fact, the kinds of cooperative systems that we are talking about here would be impossible without it.

### Developers Agree!

In 1988, a group of software vendors closely associated with IBM began developing the first crop of SAA-compliant cooperative processing applications. For over a year, each company worked independently at designing and prototyping an application. When they finally got together 18 months later to compare notes, they discovered something remarkable: every development team that had succeeded in getting an application up and running (not all did) had resorted to an emerging software technology called object-orientation. Though fully armed with SAA components and conversant with all the design models laid out in preceding chapters (though not necessarily by the names we used), these pioneering developers still found that object-orientation provided an essential missing ingredient. You will too.

It is clear now—and SAA has acknowledged as much—that certain pieces of a cooperative processing system cannot be built without OO. There are two specific areas where developers unanimously employ object concepts: for building advanced CUA user interfaces (see

Employee No: 55512

**Figure 14-1.**   *An object is data surrounded by a protective layer of code*

Chapter 9), and for designing message-based processes like the Distributed Function models we saw in Chapter 11.

Object-orientation is better known now than in 1988, and there are several shelf-feet of technical literature available. A designer should take the time to become familiar with this revolutionary technology, for it is clearly the wave of the future. This chapter offers a brief introduction to OO concepts and vocabulary, with emphasis on how object technology fits into cooperative processing development.

## Objects and Their Importance

Traditional programming divides software into **code** and **data**—two distinct entities that can be made to interact. Object-orientation takes an entirely different view of the world. In OO, code and data get fused together into new entities called "objects." An object (Figure 14-1) is a piece of data surrounded by the code that is relevant to it. For example, an employee object might have, on the inside basic data, the employee's number, name, address, and position. On the outside, it might have a layer of code that governs hiring, firing, promoting, address-changing, and salary-updating. Each of these code functions is called a "method." For another example, a scrollbar object will have, on its inside, data about this specific scrollbar's size, position, orientation, and current

Traditional: Code + Data            OO: Objects + Messages

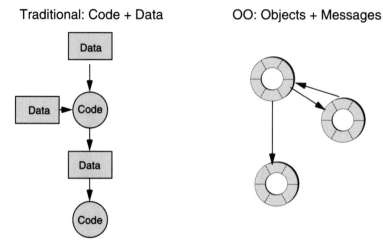

**Figure 14-2.** *Traditional programs use code and data; OO uses objects and messages*

setting, and, on the outside, such methods as value-sensing, value-setting, displaying, resizing, and so on.

Using a process called **encapsulation,** an object bundles together all the knowledge about a thing: data that represents its current **state** encapsulated in code that represents its potential **behavior**. Already we see OO moving us toward software that models objects in the real world—employees, checkbooks, parts, sales orders, videos, customers, turbine blades—and has them do recognizable things. This is a great improvement over the arcane and highly abstracted software tradition of B-trees, checkdigits, concatenated strings, non-idempotent processes, and stochastic gradients. Chapter 9 described the evolution of user interfaces back toward human-style processes after a long detour into computer-centric processes; object-orientation expresses and enables this rediscovery of the physical world.

Objects interact by sending messages to each other (Figure 14-2). A **message** is a stream of data that tells a particular object to perform a particular operation (i.e., invoke one of its methods) and furnishes whatever information might be needed to make the operation happen. A department-manager object might send a message that invokes the "Promotion" method of an employee object and tells it to bump its state up one level to senior programmer. Or our scrollbar object might send a message to the "ScrollContents" method of a window object. A message cannot approach an object's data directly; it can only communicate with the methods that form that data's protective shell. Only methods already associated with an object can be invoked; you can't send an employee object a message to "Resize" and expect anything to happen.

Whether or not you accept that the object paradigm works better at modeling the real world than does traditional procedure-oriented programming (it may take actual experience with OO programming to have this epiphany), it should be clear that this is an ideal setup for distributed systems. OO divides reality into small, self-contained entities that communicate via messages—the perfect vehicle for applications whose pieces live on far-flung heterogeneous platforms and have to interact on a moment-by-moment basis.

## Classification and Inheritance

To advance object-orientation from an interesting metaphysical system to a workable programming system, two more key concepts are necessary. Both address this obvious problem: If every separate piece of data were encapsulated with every possible action that could be performed on it, you would end up with an hopelessly fragmented universe where objects were as numerous as atoms. If each of an organization's 75,000 employees is his or her own object, how could you possibly create and keep track of that many objects, much less individually program all 75,000 with their several dozen relevant methods? The solution lies in the notions of **classification** and **inheritance**.

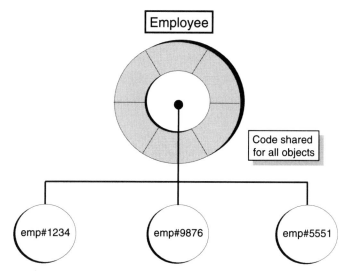

**Figure 14-3.** *Classes group objects with identical behavior*

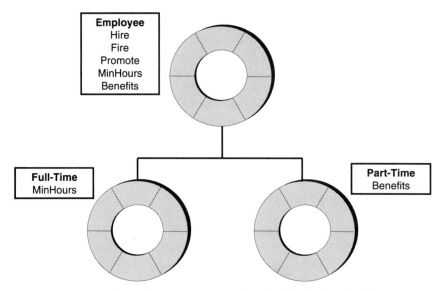

**Figure 14-4.** *Inheritance groups objects with similar behavior*

### Classification

Classification (Figure 14-3) lets us talk about our 75,000 employees as instances of a single class called "Employee." In general, a *class* groups together objects that share the same behavior. It's the class that the programmer programs, specifying just once the common behavior of all members of that class. He also specifies here exactly what data will have to be contained within each object to support that behavior. At runtime, the actual physical code lives within the class and gets applied to instances of that class as needed.

### Inheritance

Where classification allows objects to share identical behavior, inheritance (Figure 14-4) allows them to share *similar* behavior—an even more subtle achievement. OO arranges classes into hierarchies so that gross behavior gets passed down and more specific behavior gets changed. For example, the class Employee contains information about how all company employees operate. The subclasses Full-time and Part-time contain information about where the behavior of these particular types of employees differs from the general. These new subclasses only need to express their unique behavior, not repeat rules already contained in the Employee class. They *inherit* the behavior of their superclass Employee automatically. Inheritance, along with encapsulation and classification, makes OO components highly reusable and promises to alleviate much of the build-from-scratch mentality of software today.

## Objects and Cooperative Processing

The object model is winning converts throughout the application development community. Observers foresee object-orientation spreading rapidly beyond user interface architecture to databases, then revolutionizing design and analysis techniques, and eventually establishing hegemony with a full-blown, end-to-end OO software methodology.

As of today, OO gravitates toward two important areas: building state-of-the-art CUA user interfaces; and designing and building message-based, Distributed Function systems.

### Building the User Interface

The CUA chapter itemized various user interface models: Entry, Text Subset, Graphical, and Workplace. The higher-level the model, the more it requires object technology, especially object-oriented programming. If you are considering building a Graphical Model interface, object technology is strongly recommended. To build a Workplace Model interface, it is imperative.

Where the Graphical Model is concerned, even programmers who have built Graphical applications in C (as most have had to, there being no alternative when these projects started up) have used object constructs without realizing it. Look carefully at a GUI built, for example, in Windows or Presentation Manager, and you will see all of the object attributes discussed in this chapter laboriously implemented in C and the UI API. Encapsulation is built right into the window controls. Message-passing is accomplished with an explicitly coded message-processing loop; classification is done by window registration; inheritance is done by defining subclasses. These systems have installed *by hand* a full set of OO plumbing.

For the more advanced Workplace Model, jury-rigged OO plumbing is out of the question. The Workplace Model is a thoroughly object-oriented user interface, carrying the object concepts all the way out to the glass. The user sees and manipulates the very objects that the programmer programs. In an environment that deals so explicitly in objects, thoroughbred OO techniques are absolutely required. As it turns out, once you have installed an OO programming environment beneath the glass, getting these objects projected onto the glass turns out to be remarkably simple and elegant.

### Designing and Building Message-Based Systems

Organizations will typically construct their first cooperative processing applications using the simpler application models—either Distributed Presentation or Distributed Data Access. As their applications become more sophisticated, they will migrate toward the more flexible but harder-to-build Distributed Function model.

A little reflection reveals that Distributed Function applications are very close in structure to object-oriented applications. In both cases, function (a method) talks to function (another method) via messages. Once you have internalized this insight, you can start applying OO techniques—programming, design, and analysis—to building cooperative applications.

On the workstation side of a distributed system, as we have seen, OO concepts do an excellent job, especially for advanced CUA interfaces. Unfortunately, they work less well on the back end. Many host computing environments have only partial object software support or none at all. There is little compatibility between OO and the billions of lines of legacy software that runs businesses today. It seems especially hard to integrate OO into existing transaction managers. Finally, it will take a generation of training and migration support to get a critical mass of the development population on board.

We recommend a split-paradigm approach: part OO and part traditional, as shown in Figure 14-5. Split-paradigm systems are not aesthetically pleasing, but they allow you to exploit the object paradigm fully near the front of the system; and then, as you approach the back end, you can switch into the more traditional function paradigm that supports existing languages, tools, and methodologies and also ties to legacy databases and transaction managers. The back end will need to make one concession toward objects by processing messages rather than screens.

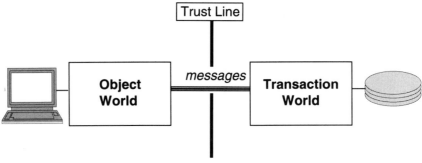

**Figure 14-5.** *The split paradigm*

The two sides of a split-paradigm system communicate by sending each other messages. Sending messages is second nature to the object side, but cumbersome to the function side. This mismatch can be addressed by assigning a certain front-end object (perhaps multiple objects) to act as a *wrapper* to the function world. The wrapper object converts a front-end message into a form that can be processed by the function side, hands it to the back end to do the work, and then returns the result. For example, a CUA workplace object simulating an order-form sends a message to an Order database wrapper, which converts the message into LU6.2 and sends it to CICS to execute a NewOrder transaction. Upon completion, a result code is sent back to end the conversation, and the wrapper object reports back to the order-form. Wrapper objects act as brokers between the object world and the function world.

A split-paradigm system usually gets developed by two separate teams. Each faces special burdens. The object developers must learn how to create the wrapper objects that "objectify" the function world behind the scenes. They also have to learn how to deal with communication mechanisms such as conversations and RPCs.

The function-world developers probably have the harder job. Although they can continue to use the same skills they have used in the past (e.g., COBOL and CICS), they have to start thinking about systems in a new way. Above all, they must learn how to handle messages rather than screens. This can be a tall order. For years, application programmers have viewed their consumer as a human sitting at a terminal. Vast amounts of their code has dealt with screen formatting, paging, and keyboard watching. Now they find themselves responding to input from an orderly process (the wrapper acting as a conduit to the front end) rather than an unpredictable person. Eventually, application programmers will see that it is easier to write message-handling programs than to write screen-handling programs, and they will happily give up all those user interface tasks that they have never been equipped to handle properly. But the readjustment will take time.

In learning to build message-based systems, function programmers are actually learning to build (very large) objects. As they become increasingly comfortable with message-passing as the normal way to connect systems together, they can start to use messaging to interconnect components within their own systems as well. Message-based systems, which by their very nature exploit a form of encapsulation, put programmers well along the road toward fully object-based systems.

## A More Aggressive Stance

How far into the application-building process can OO techniques extend? We believe that they will eventually go all the way, after many intermediate steps. The expansion of object techniques throughout applications will probably follow this scenario:

- OO extensions to traditional languages like COBOL or PL/1 will let programmers reap more of the pure programming benefits of OO.
- OO analysis and design will become second nature once developers start thinking in terms of objects. These techniques will gain acceptance as OO CASE tools become widely available.
- Farther down the line, developers can actually start the process of classification on transactions and database elements within the function environment.

Moving aggressively through these steps will not suit every organization, but the rewards match the risks. Implementing message-based systems is quite sufficient to get the object interface moving. But be prepared: Once it has a toehold, object technology tends to take root and flourish.

# Part IV

---

# Implementation Profiles

With Part III's distributed design models laid on top of the SAA componentry, we have arrived at an architecture comprehensive enough to support some actual evaluation of products and methods. The next several chapters discuss various "profiles" that you will actually use to put a system together. Some are products that you can buy (we discuss, in general, categories of products rather than specific brands); some are tools that you buy and use to build the piece that you need; some are components that you build completely from scratch. Each profile is like a recipe for a discrete piece of technology that implements the designs that enrich the architecture that supports cooperative processing.

The profiles here tend to cluster around workstation, LAN server, and connectivity requirements. Almost none addresses application-building or mainframe development issues. We are observing our charter to fill in the information and experience gap. We know from experience that many organizations find themselves in this very common situation:

- They have seen or heard about cooperative processing applications and have become convinced that these systems will be an important adjunct to their business strategy for the nineties.
- They possess strong development skills on mainframe or minis. After all, they have a long history with commercial-grade transaction processing applications.
- But they know nothing about building graphical user interfaces, much less object-oriented user interfaces. Perhaps a few energized developers have experimented with some PC- or LAN-based applications, but the organization can't see how to expand this experience to hundreds or thousands of I/S programmers.
- They haven't the faintest idea how to connect these new front ends to their back-end systems, beyond suspecting that it might have something to do with LU6.2. They may be doing a little screen-scraping (which they sense doesn't take them very far), but they are far from anything that looks like a cooperative processing architecture.

**141**

The profiles we present here acknowledge the competencies of such organizations and zero in on their weaknesses. We stop where standard application code kicks in. We concentrate on how to structure transactions, how to connect them, and what to do on the front end to drive them.

The profiles are grouped according to the general design model that they implement. For the Distributed Function model, we separate into different chapters the profiles that support the back-end piece and those that support the front end, primarily to keep each down to a manageable size.

Each profile consists of a descriptive name (the more colorful are of our own coinage), a diagram, an opinionated discussion of its value, cautions, and tips on buying or building as the case may be. An "At a Glance" summary tells in what situations the profile is most useful, the skill-sets and tools an organization will need, and a list of good points (+), drawbacks (–), and neutral characteristics (0).

# *15*

# *Distributed Presentation Profiles*

This chapter covers profiles that implement the design model where the presentation piece is distributed. They are:

• Screen-scrapers.
• Home-built screen-scrapers.

## PROFILE: SCREEN-SCRAPERS

Now that every respectable terminal-based main frame application wants an up-to-date user interface at its front end, a class of products has emerged to freshen up the look of these applications with relatively

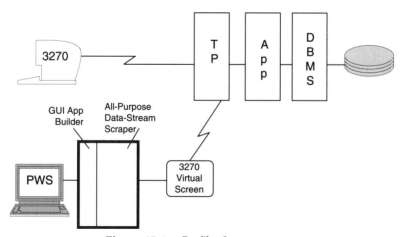

**Figure 15-1.** *Profile: Screen-scrapers*

little effort and at small expense. Easel is probably the best-known entrant in this category, though there are many others.

---

### SOME SCREEN-SCRAPERS

*Application Manager* (Intelligent Environments)
*Choreographer* (GUIdance)
*Easel* (Easel Corp.)
*Enfin* (Software Productivity International)
*I/F Builder* (Viewpoint Systems)
*InFront* (MultiSoft)
*Mozart* (Mozart)

---

We call these products screen-scrapers. As Figure 15-1 shows, they sit on the workstation, intercept terminal-bound screens, divert them to a screen buffer, scrape off the data and render it according to CUA guidelines. They also perform the same job in reverse, converting input from the workstation back into a form that the host expects and sending it on toward the back end. The host application runs unchanged, never realizing that it is talking to a workstation instead of a terminal.

A screen-scraper is actually composed of two components—one that takes care of intercepting and analyzing the old screen and one that creates and manages the new screen. Commercial screen-scrapers bundle these two functions together, but thinking of them separately comes in handy if you should ever want to build a screen-scraper of your own (see the next profile). In addition, many commercial screen-scrapers are sophisticated enough so that the two halves can work independently to handle tasks more general than screen-scraping. You could use the UI-builder half alone for any kind of user interface application, local or cooperative. Paired with another component in place of the terminal handler, it will help build message-based applications or front ends for databases.

### Split Development Cautions

Screen-scraper programming is relatively easy to learn. This ease of use lulls some designers into thinking that the screen-scraping solution is simpler than it really is. Remember that there is also a host program involved. This host program may run unchanged through the screen-scraper, but it cannot be ignored. Any time an application encompasses two different technologies controlled by two different sets of people, danger lurks. Your only safeguard is to keep the two development teams extremely well coordinated with each other.

For example, applications change. Bug reports, new features, a change in the underlying business, or even a new vision of how to line up the fields on a particular screen can require adjustments all along the line. If the developers of the host application and the screen-scraper application are in full communication with each other, this may only be an inconvenience. But it is more likely that the two teams will be based in different departments, possibly in different parts of the country. The host development team might not even know that its applications are being scraped somewhere down the line. Even if they do know, they might not remember to advise the scraper team of changes.

Larger questions arise. Who decides on feature changes that may affect the other side? Is it the screen-scraping team's job to keep adapting their front end to whatever the host developers want to do, or should there be some kind of joint decision making? Which of the two teams is the "owner" of this mixed-parentage application? Split development profiles like this one tend to reignite the two-worlds conflicts that smolder under the surface of many cooperative processing efforts.

### Evaluating Screen-Scrapers

When shopping for a screen-scraper, there are a number of things to look for:

- **What UI environments does it support?**
  Screen-scrapers are available in OS/2 PM, Windows, DOS character mode, OS/2 character mode, UNIX, and others. Some products support more than one.

- **What terminal emulation environment does it support?**
  Check that it runs in the terminal emulation environments you may need, such as 3270, 5250, or asynch terminals (and which flavor of asynch). You may even wish to have applications that scrape multiple terminal sessions simultaneously—for example, a GUI application that consolidates corporate mainframe data (through a 3270 link) with data from a departmental HP3000 (through asynch).

- **How are terminal screens captured?**
  The product should make it easy to capture the terminal screen and define it to the screen-scraper. Some earlier tools required that you specify the screens in row-column coordinates, a tedious task. More

recent tools snap a picture of the screen during an emulation session and allow you to point at fields and name them.

- **What development paradigm is used for the UI application?**
  Almost all products allow you to paint the screen using visual programming techniques. You point at a field and indicate attributes and edits—numeric or date field, table lookup of values, range checks, and so forth. Then you specify programmable rules. At this point, the screen-scraper products really start distinguishing themselves one from another. Different approaches include a simple scripting language, a 4GL-like procedural language, a rule-based language, an event-driven language, or an object-oriented language. Each user interface has different development characteristics, and each produces interfaces with a distinctive feel:

  1. *Script and procedural languages* produce applications with system-driven dialogues much like the terminal applications they are replacing. Here the dialog system leads the user through the various entry fields and options.

  2. A *rule-based language* has a similar feel, except that in some cases the order of field entry depends on the order in which the rules "fire" in their inference engine.

  3. *Event-driven and object-oriented languages* allow for user-driven, rather than system-driven, dialogs. They can accommodate more random user behavior. The user might choose to enter the last three fields, press a button, and pull down a menu option. The dialog appears to follow the user lead.

  Another factor to consider in evaluating the development paradigm is ease of development. The easiest screen-scrapers are based on the simpler procedural paradigms, while event-driven systems tend to require some mental gymnastics for application development. In the long run, developers will gravitate towards object-oriented tools which bring visual programming to large chunks of the system development process.

- **What CUA model does the screen-scraper support?**
  Different tools provide different CUA capabilities. None of them *enforces* a particular CUA level, but they can *enable* applications to be built at that level. Script and procedural languages tend to support CUA Text Subset interfaces. For the CUA Graphical level, with its ability to accommodate an unpredictable user, event-driven systems work best. Finally, the full CUA Workplace Model, with its heavy emphasis on visual objects, can only be supported by an object-oriented development paradigm.

# SCREEN-SCRAPERS AT A GLANCE

### Use This Profile for . . .

Terminal-based applications that will not be redesigned in the near future.

### Skill-Sets Required

1. Screen-scraper training (can be programmers or semiprogrammers, depending on the product).
2. CUA training.
3. System middleman to coordinate the two sides.

### Characteristics

+ **Quick user interfaces for terminal-based applications:**
  Screen-scrapers allow an organization to update old terminal applications with powerful user interfaces that take advantage of the now-widely installed PCs.

+ **Easy for developer to learn:**
  Compared to some of the other cooperative processing profiles, screen-scrapers are an easy-to-master development technique. They generally require no more learning than a new PC product—maybe a week to acquire basic skills and another week or so to get up to full speed.

− **Split skill-sets for a single application:**
  Screen-scraped applications combine two completely different technologies in a single end-to-end application. This is a recipe for trouble unless the people working at each end communicate frequently, openly, and respectfully.

− **Double jeopardy on application maintenance:**
  As host applications change, front end and back end can easily get out of synch.

+ **Good tactical solution for legacy applications:**
  Screen-scrapers can be a good tactic for reaping some of the benefits of cooperative processing without rebuilding what might be a decade-worth of legacy applications.

− **Poor strategic solution for new applications:**
  Screen-scraping is inherently short term. Writing new applications from scratch will always yield far richer connections than you could get through screen-scraping. Do not make the mistake of writing new applications the old way and then using screen-scrapers to fix them up.

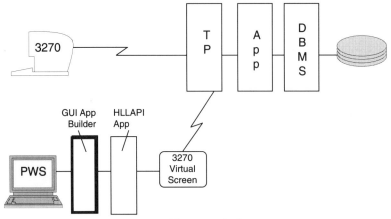

**Figure 15-2.**  *Profile: Home-built screen-scraper*

## PROFILE: HOME-BUILT SCREEN-SCRAPERS

Screen-scraper products are aggressively marketed, but you can build your own. Of course, this is true of almost any vendor-supplied component or tool, but the peculiar economics of the screen-scraper category make building your own particularly attractive.

### Building a Screen-Scraper

Figure 15-2 shows the profile diagram for a home-built screen-scraper. Like any screen-scraper, it is composed of both a UI builder and a terminal handler. If you want to go the build-it-yourself route, we recommend buying a vendor-supplied UI builder (a subsequent profile describes buying a UI builder; developing one of these is a job for a true specialist) and building the communications driver. The communications driver need not be anywhere near as sophisticated as the general-purpose screen-scraper products deliver; you can craft yours specifically for the screens your organization already supports.

Building a communications driver involves writing (in a language like C, COBOL, or REXX) a program to drive a terminal emulator. The most common emulator interface is the one used for 3270 terminals, HLLAPI (stands for High-Level Language Application Programming Interface and rhymes with "jalopy").

HLLAPI programming is an odd offshoot of a conventional programming technique that certain (rather pathological) programmers are fond of. Writing a HLLAPI program involves imagining what a terminal operator does moment-by-moment and committing it to code. For example, to perform a customer address-change transaction, the HLLAPI sequence would be something like this:

1. Put the transaction ID into the action field.
2. Put the customer number into the custno field.
3. Press the Enter key.
4. Wait for the host to paint the address-change screen.
5. Make sure that the host didn't report an error (e.g., No Such Customer) in the error message field.
6. Put the new address into the address fields.
7. Press the Enter key.
8. Make sure that the host didn't report an error.

Why would any organization choose an implementation route that involves such painful programming? The most convincing reason is to save huge amounts of money. Commercial screen-scrapers are very expensive, with prices reaching several thousand dollars per developer workstation, plus hundreds of dollars per runtime workstation. By contrast, building a screen-scraper will cost you a few hundred dollars for a commercial UI-builder development system, and you will pay no runtimes at all. Even with the cost of the expensive communication programming factored in, building can be much cheaper than buying for large-population runtime environments.

There are other advantages to a home-built screen-scraper. Standalone commercial UI builders are almost invariably superior to the UI builders packaged into screen-scraper products. You will get a nicer-looking, more powerful user interface quicker if you buy a product that devotes all its energies to building user interfaces.

Finally, in those advanced organizations that are moving toward CASE technology for their host terminal screens, home-built screen-scrapers might promise better maintenance characteristics. Once host-screen definitions are stored independent of the host environment—in a data dictionary or repository—you can build your screen-scraper to tie directly to this definition and thereby keep up with changes as they are made.

▼

## HOME-BUILT SCREEN-SCRAPERS AT A GLANCE

### Use This Profile for . . .

Terminal-based applications that will not be redesigned in the near future, where there is a large runtime population and where money is a concern.

### Skill-Sets Required

1. GUI programming.
2. HLLAPI programming to build the communications piece.
3. Middleman to coordinate teams.

### Characteristics

− **Requires specialized in-house communication skills:**
The major expense of this profile lies in building the terminal handlers. It can be tedious work, requiring a variety of skills, aptitudes, and psychopathologies.

+ **Much cheaper than a vendor-supplied screen-scraper:**
Screen-scrapers are unusually expensive pieces of software. Building your own can mean significant savings, especially for large organizations with 100+ runtime workstations.

+ **UI builders yield better user interfaces:**
None of the screen-scrapers contains a UI piece as rich as the top six commercial UI builders. The value of commercial screen-scrapers rests in their integration, not in their power.

− **Split skill-sets for a single application:**
Screen-scraped applications involve two completely different technologies in a single end-to-end application. This is a recipe for trouble unless the people working at each end communicate frequently, openly, and respectfully.

+ *Might* **be better at maintenance than a general product:**
Your own screen-scraper can be built to tie in to the updated screen definitions stored in the repository and thus keep itself up to date on any changes to the host application.

+ **Good tactical solution for legacy applications:**
Screen-scrapers can be a good tactic for getting some of the benefits of cooperative processing without rebuilding what might be a decade-worth of legacy applications.

− **Poor strategic solution for new applications:**
Screen-scraping is inherently short term. Writing new applications from scratch will always give you far richer connections than you could get through screen-scraping. Do not make the mistake of writing new applications the old way and then using screen-scrapers to fix them up.

# *16*

# *Distributed Data Access Profiles*

A small industry has grown up to provide products that facilitate access to remote and distributed databases from largely workstation-based applications. The main profiles are:

- Distributed database.
- Distributed database front end.

## PROFILE: DISTRIBUTED DATABASE

Distributed databases, shown in Figure 16-1, are one of the technological hot properties of the 1990s. Much of what is billed as "client/server computing" involves client workstations running compelling graphical environments that can reach out to specialized database servers for shared business data whenever the time comes to do community-level work. This section profiles the power and perils of distributed databases.

### *How "Distributed" Are Distributed Databases?*

Vendors of distributed database technology mean vastly different things by the term "distributed." Evaluate carefully how much distribution a product can deliver at an acceptable level of data

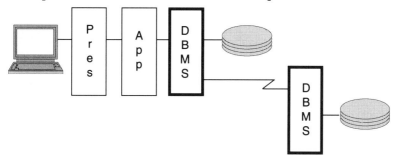

**Figure 16-1.** *Profile: Distributed database*

integrity and system performance. The question is not what function these products support, but rather what function they support *well*. Many distributed database products allow you to perform operations far beyond their ability to guarantee integrity or performance. Let the buyer beware.

### Levels of Distribution

Some help in evaluating a product's distribution competence comes from SAA, which has established standards in this area. SAA's own database strategy precisely defines four stages of distribution, though it does not yet support all of them (nor do any other vendors' products). Each level tackles an increasingly complex technical problem, and each represents a step toward complete distribution. Measure any product's claims against the SAA scale, and you will have a good idea of what you can safely expect.

- The **remote request** (Figure 16-2), the least functional and most pervasive form of distributed access now available, offers SQL access to a remote database. It does not provide any reliable form of transaction processing. In effect, every SQL statement directed to the remote database is its own transaction, and each is followed by its own implied transaction commit. Remote request remains a reliable way to inquire into a distant database.
- The **remote unit-of-work** (RUOW, Figure 16-3) introduces a limited form of reliable transaction processing. A transaction, also called a unit-of-work, requires above all that an entire set of database operations (represented in this case by SQL statements), submitted as a unit, will either fully execute or entirely abort. Under RUOW, such a transaction can be submitted to a *single* remote database with all the data integrity rules enforced as if that unit-of-work had been executed locally. The current level of SAA support for IBM's Distributed Relational Data Architecture (DRDA) achieves distributed access at the RUOW level.
- The **distributed unit-of-work** (DUOW, Figure 16-4) extends transaction processing to multiple distributed databases. It will handle

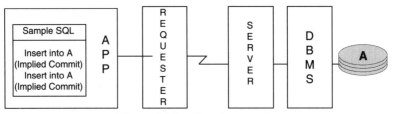

**Figure 16-2.** *Remote request*

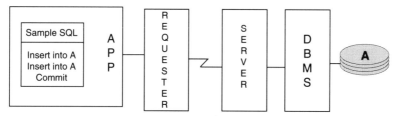

**Figure 16-3.** *Remote unit-of-work*

situations where, for example, an application executes a transaction that debits a dollar amount on a local database and credits that same amount in a remote database. Both of these operations have to execute when the transaction commits, or both of them have to be backed out when the transaction aborts. DUOW guarantees this transactional integrity, even if one of the machines or the communication line between them should fail, by requiring **two-phase commit** protocols along with the communication structures that support them. The current release level of DRDA does not support DUOW, but DB2-to-DB2 and a few third-party systems do. Here again, be careful about buying a third-party solution. For a two-phase commit algorithm to provide the high integrity that some applications require, it needs both an extremely ruggedized implementation and a strongly transaction-aware communication protocol. Not all products measure up.

• The **distributed request** (Figure 16-5) shifts from the transaction-processing priorities of the last two phases to the difficult problem of reading data from multiple distributed databases and combining that data efficiently. With the data integrity issues already solved by this point, the focus here is on efficient performance.

Achieving efficient performance across distributed relational databases presents a major challenge. Relational databases have always been notorious for sluggish performance; this is an inherent cost of the simple and easily manipulated data structures that make

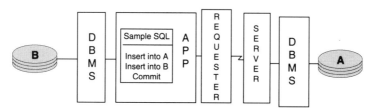

**Figure 16-4.** *Distributed unit-of-work*

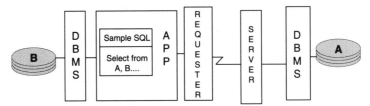

**Figure 16-5.** *Distributed request*

this kind of database so attractive. Fortunately, a number of sophisticated query-optimization techniques have evolved and have managed to raise the performance of the relational model from unacceptable to adequate. Query optimization has only been achieved for *local* relational databases, however. The kind of "global" query optimization needed for distributed databases, and even more so for databases running on heterogeneous operating systems connected by heterogeneous communication transports, is nowhere in sight. Distributed request lies well in the future, and any product that claims to offer this much distribution is, to put it kindly, exaggerating.

### The Beauty of Distributed Database

Distributed database is a wonderful technology for distributed processing. It is very easy for developers to use. There is no agonizing over where to place the cleavage line; it is already in place, between the application and the database manager. The message protocol, SQL, is so well defined and widely implemented that an application programmer can write a program without knowing whether the database is local or remote. Finally, distributed database presents a single-system image to the developer as well as to the user, which few profiles do.

Given its advantages, why don't we just advocate distributed database and forget about the other profiles? In fact, many developers do lock onto distributed database as the official platform for their entire system. This is a tempting approach, but very risky. Distributed database has a number of serious drawbacks, enumerated below, most of which grow directly out of its prime virtue—simplicity. All of the problems have at least partial solutions, but every solution involves sacrificing some of the elegant simplicity that attracts people to distributed database in the first place.

### Integrity and Performance Problems

As we have already seen, although distributed database can accomplish a job (like a complex transaction or query) quite simply, it cannot necessarily guarantee sufficient integrity or performance. Developers should proceed more carefully as their distributed database requirements become more complex. Distributed database technology works well for a spot inquiry ("lookup part description given part code") and reasonably well for a spot update ("now change the part description"), but multistep transactions demand caution. Think through the implications of each of the steps. If some steps address data in different locations from other data, make sure that your database technology is among those that support distributed transactional integrity (level DUOW) and support it *well* (few do). Finally, for the kinds of multiway, distributed queries typically done by decision-support systems, use extreme caution. Try them out, as far as you can try out what are supposed to be impromptu queries, on real-size databases.

A good developer can take steps to minimize the integrity/performance problem. You might handle distributed transactional integrity by executing a series of remote transactions with some extra application code that guarantees synchronization. You could compensate for the inefficiency around multiway distributed query by copying replicas of the tables (or portions thereof) to a single, local database. But notice that in each case, as you make the distributed database solution more robust, you give up some of its simplicity.

### The Trust Problem

On quite a different front, distributed database structures fail to observe the Trust Line disciplines we laid out in Chapter 4. Many system builders exploiting distributed database technology have built a simple application on the client workstation and had it address the community data on some upstream database engine. But since application function can be an enterprise asset as surely as the data in the database, this architecture poses significant trust problems. If security and integrity are important in your application, you should not put an enterprise asset like trusted business logic on an untrusted workstation.

Here, again, there are a number of alternatives. You could just forget about trust; some applications can do without this kind of protection. You could make the workstation trusted, provided that the end user will not mind the loss of freedom. Or you could move some of the application logic up to a trusted server, as Figure 16-6 shows. In this last

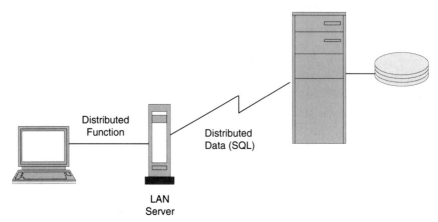

**Figure 16-6.** *Moving application logic upward into a trusted region*

scenario, protect the application asset by moving its critical parts to a trusted environment and using a Distributed Function arrangement involving an untrusted workstation. This solution is quite powerful but, predictably, it complicates the "simple" distributed database.

### The Overloaded Seam Problem

Another cost of distributed database grows directly out of its very nature. When data lives in one place and the code that works on the data lives somewhere else, the connection between them can get phenomenally busy. The communication traffic over this seam, measured both in number of interactions and in volume of data, far exceeds the traffic of, for example, the application-to-presentation seam. And the actual cost of that seam, in both money and performance, increases dramatically as the communication transport shifts from a relatively cheap and fast local area network to a slow and expensive wide area network. The result is that distributed databases get expensive as the data volume goes up and exceedingly expensive as the communication distance increases. As a leading distributed database pioneer admitted to us: "Distributed databases work best when the two machines are about 5 feet apart."

And this is just for the *average* application mix. Certain atypical, but still frequent, cases can be astronomically worse. Consider an application that needs to compute a standard deviation on the Quantity-On-Hand field over some 100,000 rows in a remote table. Using a Distributed Data Access request to retrieve that data and compute the value locally is vastly more expensive than using a Distributed Function request that sends a message to a partner process on the remote machine telling it do the work in application code and send the answer back.

Here, too, there is a solution. Real-world applications that exploit distributed databases should do so in conjunction with Distributed Function processing. Distributed Function can directly address the problem of the busy application-to-database seam by taking the chunk of the application that most frequently talks to the database and relocating it right next to the data. Notice how this recommendation leads right back to the insights of object-orientation: You gain both software power and performance by surrounding data (the remote database) with a layer of code (the application that works on it) and then activating it by sending messages to the code.

A number of vendor products address this need to move function into the database and subsequently execute that function from the client. Solutions include:

- **Stored functions** written in a standard language like C or COBOL that can be invoked by the remote client (like DARI in OS2/EE).
- **Stored procedures** written in a proprietary 4GL.
- **Triggers**, special kinds of stored procedures that can be executed automatically on some database event ("edit a field value before putting it into the database").
- **SQL extensions** that add logic to the database access language so that conditional transactions can be formulated and executed without frequent communication interactions.

All four techniques are useful for moving function into the database. However, none is architected. In adopting one or another, you risk not only losing portability but also finding yourself unable to adapt to new database standards as they emerge. Future extensions to SQL will solve the problem definitively with *architected* stored procedures and triggers, and you will want to be in a position to take advantage.

### Distributed Database as a Component, Not a Platform

The above problems should not discourage you from using distributed database, which is a powerful component in the cooperative processing tool kit, but they should alert you to the dangers of treating distributed database as a distribution platform. Developers who rely on distributed database exclusively are heading right for performance, integrity, trust and expense problems. If you use distributed database in conjunction with other application models, especially Distributed Function, you will be able to take advantage of its strengths and mitigate its weaknesses.

▼

---

## DISTRIBUTED DATABASE AT A GLANCE

### Use This Profile for . . .

Virtually all cooperative processing applications that have to access remote data.

### Skill-Sets Required

1. Relational database and SQL skills.
2. Database architect who understands the complexities of various database configurations.

### Characteristics

+ **Single system-image for the developer:**
  Distributed database allows developers to write programs that can be either local or distributed with no extra coding.

0 **Product integrity and performance constraints:**
  Distributed database simplicity may be offset by integrity and performance constraints.

− **Splitting code and data may be harmful to your mental health:**
  Distributed database encourages thinking about application code separately from the data that it works on. This type of thinking is exactly what object-orientation is trying to cure. Try instead to create code wrappers that can "objectivity" the view of the data.

---

## PROFILE: DISTRIBUTED DATABASE FRONT END

A number of products allow developers quickly to build graphical user interface applications that sit on the front end of SQL-speaking databases, as shown in Figure 16-7. Because these products are integrated with both the database manager and with the UI builder, it is easy to build applications that glue these two end-points together. For example, an entry field can be visually connected with a database table and field to indicate what field entry goes into what part of the database.

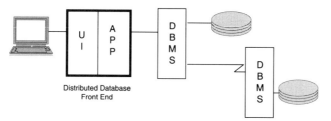

**Figure 16-7.** *Profile: Distributed database front end*

## SOME DISTRIBUTED DATABASE FRONT ENDS

*Easel* (Easel Corp.)
*Choreographer* (GUIdance)
*SQL Windows* (Gupta Technologies)
*SQL-Forms* (Oracle Corp.)
*PowerBuilder* (PowerSoft Corp.)
*Enfin* (Software Productivity International)

Some products, like Gupta's SQL Windows, can front-end a variety of database products. Others, like SQL-Forms from Oracle, are database-specific and are provided by the database vendors themselves. Still others are being introduced by screen-scraper vendors, like Easel, who are diversifying into other application models.

This profile tends to be appropriate only for simple user access to a database. Seek out more sophisticated application structures if your application requires more flexible function placement (placing trusted edits in an upstream server, for example), maintenance by a team of developers, or architected standards for business logic.

## DISTRIBUTED DATABASE FRONT END AT A GLANCE

### Use This Profile for . . .

End-user-constructed applications. The value of these tools diminishes for commercial-grade applications.

### Skill-Sets Required

1. Relational database and SQL skills.
2. Front-end tool training.

### Characteristics

+ **Applications can be built quickly:**
The built-in UI piece, plus direct integration with the database, lets you make connections quickly and easily.

− **Inappropriate for richer application models:**
Useful especially for simpler user access to a database or as an inquiry component to a larger system.

+ **Single system-image for the developer:**
Distributed database allows developers to write programs that can be either local or distributed with no extra coding.

0 **Product integrity and performance constraints:**
Distributed database simplicity may be offset by integrity and performance constraints.

# 17

# *Distributed Function Back Ends*

A number of the most useful profiles offer various ways of implementing the Distributed Function design model.

Distributed Function systems offer the most flexibility, but tend to be the hardest to build. Object-orientation has recently offered conceptual tools—and is gradually delivering real working tools—to make development easier. As of today, OO tools are useful primarily on the front end, as we will see in the next chapter. The back ends of Distributed Function systems, covered in this chapter, still require largely traditional development approaches. The major job here is to arrange for back-end applications to handle the messages coming in from the front ends. Each back-end profile has to be matched up with a compatible front-end profile (the front-end chapter follows).

Throughout this chapter, we include pseudocode fragments simply to give a sense of the architectural implications of a profile. For actual coding techniques for database access, communication, transaction management, resource recovery, concurrency, and so on, look to the literature on particular products.

Back-end profiles for Distributed Function systems are:

- Communication-aware transactions.
- Capsule transactions.
- Function dispatcher.
- CICS/OS2.
- Remote procedure call.
- Case-generated transactions

## General Considerations for Back-End Profiles

Two general development imperatives apply across all the back-end profiles that we will look at. You should be sure to:

- Avoid presentation dependencies in your code.
- Keep code as portable as possible.

It is worth taking the time to understand the reasons for each before we start looking at specific profiles.

### Avoid Presentation Dependencies

The vast majority of host programmers have learned the trade of writing application code that sits between screen and database. Consequently, most large organizations have millions of lines of code that looks like this:

Paint movie selection screen onto terminal.

Get movie title from user.

Get movie data from the database.

Put movie data into fields on the screen.

Get any changed fields from the screen.

Edit the changes.

Write the new fields into the database.

Report to the screen the results of the database write.

Notice the constant shift among statements that (1) talk to the terminal, (2) talk to the database, (3) do some computing. These strands are so intermingled that if, for example, this program was written to interface to a 3270 terminal, a strong built-in 3270 dependency would be scattered all through it.

Figure 17-1 shows presentation handling hopelessly entangled with transaction handling. Code so pervaded by presentation dependency presents a real obstacle to rich cooperative processing systems. It is also difficult to reengineer without significant human involvement. This kind of code guarantees screen-scrapers a long and useful life.

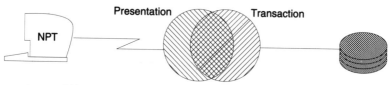

**Figure 17-1.** *Old way to write code: Presentation and transaction logic intermingled*

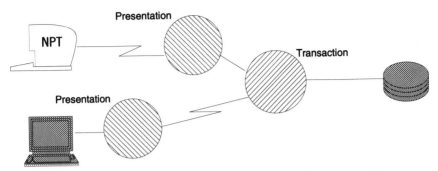

**Figure 17-2.** *New way to write code: Separate presentation dependencies*

Figure 17-2 shows the way to write new code from now on. Break it up into discrete modules. Put all of the data handling, whether database access or business logic, into separate modules from the presentation code. Under this plan, the previous transaction would yield these "pure" data-handling transactions:

GetMovie Method:

Receive GetMovie message with movie title.

Get movie data from database.

Return movie data.

ChangeMovie Method:

Receive ChangeMovie message with movie data.

Lookup movie data.

Edit the data.

If data ok, update the database.

Return result code.

As developers start building message-based back ends they will make some interesting discoveries:

- Transactions become drastically simpler once they are freed of screen support (especially multipage screens).
- Transactions get smaller. These smaller chunks will prove to be far more reusable in other contexts (e.g., new projects).

- Message-driven transactions can be driven by completely different computing environments. For example, a merged or acquired company may wish to submit movie changes from its VAX into the same transaction. All it needs to do is mimic the message format and communication protocol.

---

## PRESENTATION ISOLATION FOR CICS DEVELOPERS

Interest in cooperative processing runs high in the CICS community, which numbers some 30,000 shops. Presentation isolation has special implications for CICS developers.

Removing presentation dependencies means more than just isolating all of the EXEC statements that refer to the terminal screen. There is also the structural dependency, called **pseudo-conversational programming**, that most shops require to keep the system running efficiently.

In building transactions for cooperative processing, consider pseudo-conversationality as another presentation dependency. This structure has no place in the data-handling transaction. However, the 3270-terminal-handling module shown in Figure 17-2 should be pseudo-conversational.

---

### Keep Code Portable

Portable code has long been considered an excellent practice, the idea being that the system might some day be moved to other environments. But portability has a more immediate value for a cooperative processing system, where *portability equals tuneability*. Where a piece of function lives relative to other function or data affects overall system performance more than any other factor does. Should the EditEmployee method be next to the back-end database, right under the user interface, or somewhere in between? Should it perhaps be broken apart or replicated? To keep options open on questions like these, you have to have portable code.

The most obvious variable for achieving portability is the language the business logic is written in. Most shops should write their most portable business logic in COBOL, which has efficient implementations on all the SAA platforms as well as the largest population of trained programmers (98% of all commercial I/S programmers know COBOL).

This does not mean that the entire system must be written in COBOL. You may, for example, use Smalltalk to build a powerful OOUI, C to build multithreaded OS/2 servers, and PL/1 to create mainframe-server scaffolding. But when you get to the central code that defines the business problems—the AddEmployee, CompensationChange, New-SalesOrder, CreditCheck, MovieLookup, and so forth—use the language that your platforms and development teams can support. This is not always as easy as it would seem, for in a mixed-language environment there is always the temptation to use a platform-specific language for what needs to be an enterprisewide function. Project leaders should remind developers to keep organizational assets portable.

Languages are not the only factors that affect portability. Different operating environments tend to provide different services for memory management, exceptions, time and date, and others, and these differences retard portability. Better isolate them to small, environment-specific modules until they become standardized.

## PROFILE: COMMUNICATION-AWARE TRANSACTION

Given the SAA materials available, the most obvious kind of transactions to build are those that combine (1) application algorithms written in an SAA language, with (2) SAA Database Interface to talk to the database, and (3) SAA Communication Interface (CI, or CPIC) to talk to the front end or to other distributed elements. This profile (Figure 17-3) is always explicitly aware of the communications environment in which it is operating.

How would you implement the ChangeMovie transaction mentioned earlier under such a profile? Assume that a front-end process has determined a need to update movie information. It could create an LU6.2 message containing the movie title to be changed, plus the list of fields to be changed, and a communications-aware transaction like the following would respond from the back end:

Accept the incoming conversation (CPIC: CMACCP).

Receive the incoming data (CPIC: CMRCV).

Lookup movie data (SQL: SELECT).

Edit the new data.

If data ok, update the database (SQL: UPDATE).

Send result code back (CPIC: CMSEND).

Deallocate the conversation (CPIC: CMDEAL).

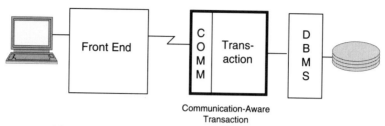

**Figure 17-3.** *Profile: Communication-aware transaction*

This type of transaction is called communication-aware because it contains explicit communications statements that send the incoming messages from a communications line and write the outgoing result back to the communications line. Remember that the Communications Interface accommodates an almost infinite number of communication protocol combinations; we show a simple request-reply conversation here because these are used so frequently.

Such transactions will be portable to all environments that support the SAA CI. Currently, or in the near term, these include CICS, MVS/APPC, VM, AS/400, OS/2, and IMS/TM (with a detour through MVS/APPC). CPIC has been picked up by other standards groups and coalitions and is finding its way to a variety of platforms. Unfortunately, there are still a great many other environments to which CPIC interfaces are not portable, most notably "skinny client" environments (those with reduced speed, memory, and resources) such as Windows, DOS, or other workstation clients like Macintoshes. Some older CPIC implementations do not even allow communications within the same environment, and some of the newer ones that do allow it load on enormous overhead. This is a shame, for it is often useful to write transactions that can be used locally or remotely without a lot of preplanning. The next profile solves this problem.

▼

**COMMUNICATION-AWARE TRANSACTIONS AT A GLANCE**

**Use This Profile for . . .**

Environments that choose to standardize on a single communication protocol for Distributed Function applications. Note that this decision will restrict future options.

**Skill-Sets Required**

1. Training in communication programming.

## Characteristics

+ **Portable to environments with CPIC support:**
  As long as there is a single communication API (like CPIC), this profile might be a reasonable choice.

− **Nonportable to many environments—even the "local" environment:**
  By building the communication selection into the application, this profile limits future choices. It may even prevent you from using this code in environments where it needs to be executed locally.

− **Communications explicit to programmer:**
  Communication-aware transactions require the application programmer to get explicitly involved with communications, which most would rather not do. Communications programming is tricky. The error paths are much more complex than in conventional software. Worst of all, strong cohesion is required between the two communicating software modules: if process B decides to "turn the line around," process A had better be watching for it.

+ **Any kind of communication sequence can be created:**
  Most sophisticated cooperative processing systems will retain areas that call for specialized and complex interactions beside simple request-reply. Transaction forwarding, replica management, event broadcasting, and software distribution are a few examples of where this profile will continue to find an audience.

## PROFILE: CAPSULE TRANSACTION

The transaction style that we call "capsule" (Figure 17-4) will be the workhorse structure of most of the Distributed Function profiles. It solves both the problems that arise with communication-aware transactions (CPIC statements are nonportable; programmers don't like doing communications) in the simplest possible way: by lopping off the communication statements. Data comes from a parameter list handed to the module when it is called.

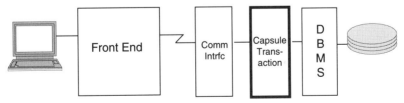

**Figure 17-4.** *Profile: Capsule transaction*

The capsule version of the ChangeMovie transaction looks like this:

Lookup movie data of title in parameter input area.

Edit the new data from parameter input area.

If data ok, update the database.

Place result in parameter output area and return.

You may notice that the capsule transaction is not as full a profile as the previous ones. It is really a subprofile that provides an extremely useful coding structure for building Distributed Function cooperative processing systems.

In fact, the capsule transaction is simply the business kernel of a transaction with all external interface information removed. It is usually executed as a subroutine to some higher-level module, often called a **scaffold**, that does the interface work. Since subroutines tend to be written with a single-entry single-exit protocol, the capsule transaction is limited to handling request-reply interactions characteristic of client/server relationships. This limitation poses no problem, for such interactions are by far the most widely used in cooperative processing systems.

Using a capsule transaction typically involves building a scaffold to enfold the transaction in the interface protocol of choice. For example, a CPIC scaffold supporting a communication protocol identical to the last profile's ChangeMovie transaction would look like this:

Accept the incoming conversation (CPIC: CMACCP).

Receive the incoming data (CPIC: CMRCV).

Move the input data into the parameter input area.

Call "ChangeMovie" using parameter (capsule version).

Move the parameter output area to a result buffer.

Send result code back (CPIC: CMSEND).

Deallocate the conversation (CPIC: CMDEAL).

Take another example: supporting this same transaction on an OS/2 LAN server to be called by a Microsoft Windows client. A convenient and lightweight interface technique involves using a "named pipe" interface to move the message over the LAN. The named pipe scaffold would look like this:

Make a named pipe with a predefined name.

Connect the pipe (wait for the client message).

Read the message from the pipe.

Move the input data into the parameter input area.

Call "ChangeMovie" using parameter (capsule version).

Move the parameter output area to a result buffer.

Write the result code to the pipe.

Disconnect the pipe.

You could erect similar scaffolds for other protocols like Netbios, Novell IPX/SPX, and minicomputer asynch streams. We have even seen HLLAPI-driven transports that move messages (rather than screens) over an LU2 (3270) interface.

In certain environments, such as DOS or OS/2, you could eliminate the scaffold entirely and link the capsule transaction as a dynamic link library (DLL). The capsule transaction would become a true subroutine to a workstation process, making it possible, for example, to write edit transactions that can run anywhere in the cooperative environment.

### Building Capsule Transactions

It is not hard to build a capsule transaction. If you are using COBOL, simply build a standard subroutine that looks like this:

```
identification division.
program-id. ChangeMovie.

data division.
linkage section.
01 parameter-area.
   10 input-area.
      copy input-record.
   10 output-area.
      copy output-record.

procedure division using parameter-area.
   ... your business logic here ...
   goback.
```

The only tricky part is the linkage section. We strongly recommend, for portability reasons, that a capsule transaction pass only a single parameter. Notice that there is a single level-01 record called "parameter-area" (the name here is irrelevant). Since multiple values are almost always passed, they should be grouped under the single level-01 parameter. Here we show input and output subrecords. Each has a COPY statement for pulling in the fields required.

Assuming that the procedure division does not contain environment-specific code (which should be further isolated to a separate service module), this form of capsule transaction will prove extremely portable.

---

▼

### CAPSULE TRANSACTIONS AT A GLANCE

#### Use This Profile for . . .

General purpose, portable Distributed Function programming.

#### Skill-Sets Required

1. Training in use of standard capsule template.
2. A master programmer to build the scaffold code.

#### Characteristics

+ **Extreme portability of business logic:**
  This profile allows you to move the application portions of a cooperative processing system almost anywhere with little or no conversion.

+ **Encourages small code modules:**
  Capsule transactions foster the notion of small, well-encapsulated, atomic blocks of function. They will serve well in terms of program maintenance and will lay the groundwork for some subsequent profiles.

− **Limited to request-reply interactions:**
  Not all distributed interactions should be client-requesting to server-responding, but the vast majority are. This profile handles them very easily.

− **Requires organizationwide standards for development:**
  Capsule transactions add architecture to the application-building process. This solution calls for a great deal of discipline, cooperation, and commitment among the people implementing it.

---

### PROFILE: FUNCTION DISPATCHER

The transactions that we have created up until now perform their single fragment of business logic and return the results. But real-world

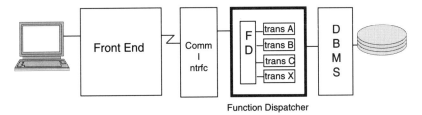

**Figure 17-5.**  *Profile: Function dispatcher*

applications package up dozens—or hundreds, or thousands—of these atomic transactions. Some environments, like MVS/APPC, support frameworks that can maintain and dispatch large numbers of individual transactions; other environments, like OS/2, require that you do more of the transaction packaging work yourself. Even when not required, there are benefits to building a transaction package—that is, a function dispatcher—of your own.

Figure 17-5 shows a simple function dispatcher. It lives between the scaffold code and a whole set of capsule transactions, both of which were covered in the previous profile. Every message that comes in contains an additional field called a **selector**, usually glued to the front of the message. This field identifies which capsule transaction should be fired. The function dispatcher performs the following general operation:

Get the incoming message.

Put the selector field into a holding area.

Move the rest of the message into the parameter input area.

If selector not in function table return Error.

Call the module named in the selector using the parameter.

When it's done, move the parameter output to a result buffer.

Return a reply message.

In its simplest form, a function dispatcher is little more than a message parser and a "case" statement. This message-handling plumbing looks very much like the code that implements encapsulation in object-oriented systems. In fact, one way to look at a function dispatcher is that it allows you to create gargantuan objects.

Figure 17-6, which refines the function dispatcher, reveals that this structure has deeper purposes than just packaging transactions. In the original function-dispatcher diagram, an incoming message whose

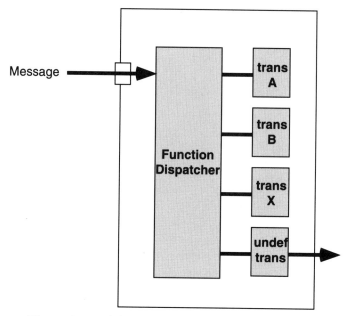

**Figure 17-6.**  *A function dispatcher with a message drain*

selector had no matching function was considered an error. In this refined version, an unmatched message gets drained out the back of the function dispatcher and continues upstream. Implementing server cascades (Figure 17-7) thus becomes possible. If the message hits the last server unresolved, only then is an error returned.

Server cascades implement a form of inheritance. You can install transactions that reflect enterprise policy on your upstream host and still provide for these policies to be overridden by departmental policy

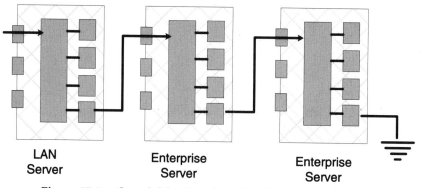

**Figure 17-7.**  *Cascaded function dispatchers implement inheritance*

installed closer downstream. Consider a NewHire transaction that needs to serve two purposes in two different places. The code to add it to the database may be back on the enterprise host, directly updating DB2. But your department needs the data as well for a study of local hiring practices you have been asked to do. As the NewHire message flows through the departmental server, a local NewHire transaction can copy the relevant data fields to a departmental database, then reinsert the message upstream for subsequent processing.

▼

## OS/2 SERVER DEVELOPERS: THINK MULTIPROCESS

To implement scaffolds and function dispatchers on a full-scale transaction manager like CICS, your code modules can pretty much follow the pseudocode provided in these sections. This is because CICS is architected to give to multiple simultaneous consumers (users on terminals, or processes) the impression that each is the sole owner of the environment. You can code the same way, of course, when writing these facilities on a client workstation where the process really *does* control the environment.

The problem comes with writing such code on a LAN server that services multiple simultaneous user processes. When you write this same code for OS/2, UNIX, or other preemptive multitaskers (don't even think about trying to write server code on a singletasking environment), you have to do a little more work.

Experienced OS/2 programmers will quickly come up with an initial solution: Make the scaffold code multithreaded. When a message arrives, a thread of execution can be unblocked to satisfy the message request. A number of issues attend multithreaded OS/2 servers, and these have been thoroughly documented. Unfortunately none of this documentation addresses the added complexity that appears frequently in cooperative processing.

The reason for this complexity is that certain communications and database products have constraints on thread and process usage. For example, OS/2 database managers allow one database connection per process, no matter how many threads the process creates. The best solution is to implement a multiprocess server, rather than just a multithreaded server, so that each server process can support an open database connection.

Figure 17-8 shows the general design of a multiprocess server. When the server is started, it spawns multiple instances of the process that contains the function dispatcher and its set of capsule transactions. The number of processes in this pool can be a configuration parameter. A thread manages the communications events. When a message arrives, it takes its place in the

Request_Queue. Another thread marries an available request with an available process. The process is then unblocked to handle the request. (For an in-depth examination of this technique, see Robert Lindsay's article, "Multiple Conversation OS/2 Server Using IBM SAA," *IBM Personal Systems Developer* [Summer 1991].)

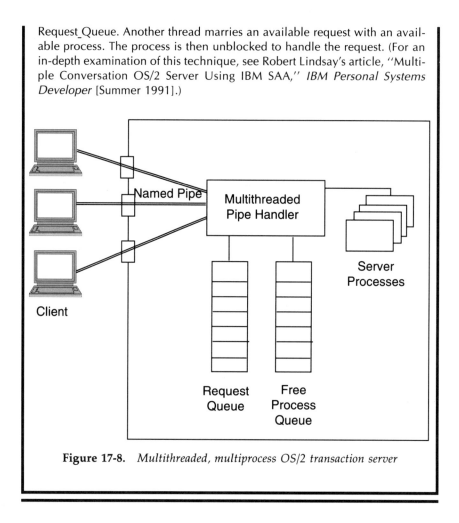

**Figure 17-8.** *Multithreaded, multiprocess OS/2 transaction server*

Step back a moment and you will see that the function dispatcher plays a pivotal roll in any cooperative processing system. Its job is to assemble a package of transactions, each with a corresponding message to drive it. The aggregate of all the messages that the function dispatcher takes becomes, in essence, the protocol for messages coming from the front end to the back end. We have here the "negotiated settlement" incarnate. The set of messages that drives the function dispatcher embodies in concrete (actually in code) form the contract for data and services negotiated between the user community and the glass house back in Chapter 4.

▼

## FUNCTION DISPATCHERS AT A GLANCE

### Use This Profile for . . .

Building a standard framework for capsule transactions.

### Skill-Sets Required

1. Master programmer to build function dispatcher.
2. Application programmers to build capsule transactions.

### Characteristics

+ **Embodies the crux of the "negotiated settlement":**
  A function dispatcher creates a single control-point where interface issues can be negotiated and implemented.

+ **Packages a family of capsule transactions:**
  A function dispatcher provides a portable wrapper for a family of capsule transactions.

+ **Adds a form of encapsulation and inheritance to transactions:**
  A function dispatcher adds increased plumbing to handle message-based applications. Although this technique works only at the module level, it does offer some object benefits "in the large."

− **Requires organizationwide standards for development:**
  Function dispatchers add architecture to the application-building process. This solution calls for a great deal of discipline, cooperation, and commitment among the people implementing it.

## PROFILE: CICS/OS2

This is the only profile limited to a single type of computing environment, namely CICS (Figure 17-9). CICS has been extended to

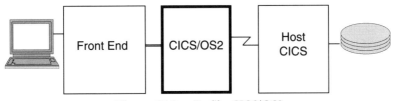

**Figure 17-9.** *Profile: CICS/OS2*

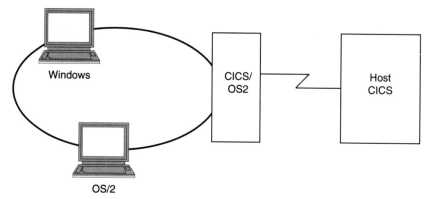

**Figure 17-10.** *CICS/OS2 on the LAN server*

communicate to remote mainframe environments, so important distributed concepts are already built in. Furthermore, the popular CICS
transaction manager (30,000 sites and hundreds of thousands of applications) has been ported to OS/2 and PCDOS and should soon appear on
the AS/400 and RS/6000 as well. By hitching a ride on all this built-in
distribution functionality, you can get good distribution quite cheaply.

### How Does a Distributed CICS Work?

Figure 17-10 shows a typical configuration of a CICS/OS2 transaction.
Notice that CICS/OS2 is shown as a transaction server located on the
LAN. This seems to be a particularly useful place for it, since the
application business logic can be located on a trusted server, can be
written by garden-variety COBOL/CICS programmers, and still can be
readily available over a high-speed, cheap path to skinny clients.

Contrast this configuration with the one IBM tends to recommend.
Their configuration prefers CICS/OS2 on each client. This conserves all
the system power and transparency of distributed CICS, but at a considerable expense in workstation size and loss of workstation
heterogeneity.

No matter which configuration you choose, CICS distributed features
work pretty much the same way. In order of their importance to cooperative processing, the features are as follows:

- **Distributed program link**, new to CICS/OS2, heads the list. It
  extends the CICS LINK verb that allows calling a transaction as a
  subroutine. Merely indicating that a linked program is remote in

the program processing table (PPT) transfers execution to the remote program, including all data conversions as system boundaries are crossed. What you have is a built-in CICS remote procedure call.

- **Function shipping** makes it possible for various CICS resources (files, transient storage, temporary queues, sync point requests, interval control) to live on a remote CICS. Since they are defined in resource tables outside of the actual application, the application never needs to know whether the data is local or remote. Function can be shipped between workstations or between workstation and host. Note that this feature implements the Distributed Data Access application model discussed in Chapter 11.

- **Distributed transaction processing** refers to the CICS command-level verbs for controlling conversational communications (via LU6.2) between remote CICS regions or between a CICS region and any other program that speaks LU6.2. Why is this verb set included here when we have already recommended the SAA CPIC interface for controlling conversations? History. The CICS DTP (Distributed Transaction Processing) verbs predate CPIC by several years; in fact, CICS-CPIC is available only in the very latest version. If you have the choice, use CPIC for portability reasons. Whether you use DTP verbs or CPIC verbs, the resultant on-the-wire protocol is the same, so there is no problem with a CPIC transaction holding a conversation with a DTP transaction.

- **Asynchronous processing** enables an application program to initiate transactions on a remote system using the CICS START command. It is called asynchronous because the STARTing transaction does not wait for the remote transaction to complete, but continues running.

- **Transaction routing** allows a transaction on one CICS region to cause a transaction in a remote region to execute. This capability tends to be most relevant for terminal-based transactions connecting to a remote region. Uses in cooperative processing seem limited to such things as Automatic Transaction Initiation.

One word of caution: Due to current constraints on the communication environment, CICS/OS2 uses sync level 1 (CONFIRM) rather than the mainframe-supported sync level 2 (SYNCHRONIZE) logic that supports two-phase commit. Consequently, a familiar warning applies. This environment is suitable for remote transactions ("update remote resources"), but for distributed transactions ("update resources in multiple locations with integrity") it has dangerous gaps.

## Using Distributed CICS to Build Cooperative Applications

The abundant tool support behind CICS/OS2 seems to offer many possibilities for building cooperative applications. For example, you could use distributed program link to invoke the remote transaction that updates the database. You could function-ship tables that you need to access. In rare cases, you could even use distributed transaction processing to create more sophisticated interactions than the request-reply interaction defined in distributed program link.

Even with all these features available, we strongly recommend using this profile in combination with the preceding profiles of capsule transactions and function dispatchers. A cascaded function dispatcher resides on both the LAN server and the enterprise servers. A simple distributed program link joins them together. Function shipping provides auxiliary support for Distributed Data Access.

You should consider this approach even when alternatives are available because of the radical portability that capsule transactions provide. Even in this configuration, you still might want to replicate some of these transactions on the workstation in a non-CICS environment. The capsule transactions will not know the difference. The function dispatcher component allows you to implement the encapsulation and inheritance properties described in the last section, which are also quite useful in this environment.

### Handling the User Interface

To use CICS/OS2 for cooperative processing, ignore the built-in CICS user interface verbs. They are far too terminal-oriented. We advocate replacing them with state-of-the-art UI building languages or tools.

There are two possibilities for interfacing UI-builders to CICS. Since CICS/OS2 supports full LU6.2 communication, clients that speak LU6.2 can talk to it that way. Alternatively, CICS/OS2, in its later releases, supports an External Call Interface (ECI), an API that non-CICS programs can call. For running CICS/OS2 on a LAN server, some communication scaffold (e.g., for a named pipe) can enfold CICS/OS2 and CALL it, specifying a transaction to run plus a parameter area.

### CICS/OS2 AT A GLANCE

**Use This Profile for . . .**

CICS shops who want an easy way to provide solid connectivity to the host.

---

### Skill-Sets Required

1. Knowledge of CICS distributed capabilities.

### Characteristics

+ **Developer can avoid communication responsibilities:**
  Linked CICS environments provide numerous facilities that can simplify building a distributed system. Application programmers can avoid most of the exigencies of distributed systems.

+ **Moves split system-image nearer to glass:**
  Although this protocol still imposes a split system-image on the developer, the traditional CICS paradigm extends to near the front.

− **CICS dependent:**
  This profile is useful only for CICS shops and particularly those CICS shops willing to get their developers involved in workstation development.

− **More system overhead on the workstation:**
  CICS/OS2 is a hefty environment that adds extra overhead to the workstation. It may not be the ideal choice for every workstation. On the other hand, it can be a useful environment for the trusted LAN server.

---

## PROFILE: REMOTE PROCEDURE CALL

Remote procedure call (RPC) has gained a reputation as a near-ideal form of linkage in distributed computing (RPC appears in its communication-model incarnation in Chapter 13). The RPC (Figure 17-11) is widely used in the UNIX community, and a variety of third-party products make it available on most commercial computing platforms.

Particularly important to the SAA community has been the selection of the Open Software Foundation/Distributed Computing Environment (OSF/DCE) to become the SAA standard RPC. The result will be a

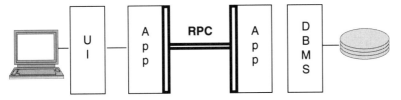

**Figure 17-11.** *Profile: Remote procedure call*

widespread cross-platform RPC that will allow applications to CALL from any SAA, AIX, or OSF platform to any other.

Be aware that early versions will not be transactional. You can expect that each CALL will act independently from every other without any commit scope. Attribute this to RPC's origins in the UNIX community, which deals predominantly with *conversational* applications rather than *transactional* applications. Conversational applications demand much less transactional integrity, so even the communication transport on which the OSF/DCE is based, TCP/IP, has no transactional support. Third-party vendors, notably Transarc, are pioneering in distributed transactional components. We expect these or similar components eventually to be architected.

As with distributed CICS, you can transparently (to the program and programmer) route a CALL to either a local or remote function. But do not let the ease of remote procedure calls lull you into a false sense of complacency. Discipline yourself to be aware of when you will be crossing communication lines, for, even though an RPC looks the same as a local call, the RPC typically costs a thousand times more. For the foreseeable future, while performance and integrity issues remain dominant themes of distribution, you should resist viewing an RPC as "transparently" as the technology allows. We again recommend the function dispatcher plus capsule transactions as the application architecture of choice, whether the distribution vehicle is a communication link, a call, or an RPC.

▼

## REMOTE PROCEDURE CALL AT A GLANCE

### Use This Profile for . . .

Powerful vendor-independent client/server connectivity.

### Skill-Sets Required

1. Knowledge of how to configure RPC tables and directories.

### Characteristics

+ **Relieves developer of explicit communication responsibilities:** Architected RPCs provide the best linkage mechanism yet. They allow function distribution that is reliable, location transparent, and authenticated against suspicious partners.

+ **Platform-independent over a wide population:**
  RPC standards enable function distribution over a much wider range of systems than do other types of connectivity.

− **Watch for integrity problems:**
  Versions of architected RPCs available in the immediate future will not be transactional.

− **Watch for performance problems:**
  The RPC's greatest strength, its location transparency, can be its greatest weakness. It remains important to design systems that use RPCs for distribution only. Following the guidelines for message-based systems established here, whether you use RPCs or not, will produce more resilient, more distributable systems.

## PROFILE: CASE-GENERATED TRANSACTIONS

Back in the SAA CPI chapter (7), we asserted that CASE technology would take on much of the development burden, replacing traditional programming languages. Here we see how CASE tools can play a specialized but important role as an implementation profile (Figure 17-12).

CASE technology has evolved from tools designed for building stand-alone business applications with dumb terminal interfaces. Over the past few years IBM's AD/Cycle has made a priority of refitting these tools for cooperative processing. In fact, CASE tool vendors have now widely exploited cooperative processing as the technology base for the tools themselves.

To use CASE technology for building cooperative processing systems, keep your expectations modest. Think of CASE as the tool set for building capsule transactions *only*. Do not try to use it for other cooperative processing components such as function dispatchers or front-end support. The capsule transaction is pure business logic and database access. Current CASE tool technology can help the designer to understand the business and can analyze, design, and even generate the code

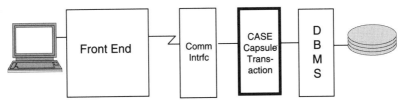

**Figure 17-12.** *Profile: CASE-generated transactions*

for this portion of the application. Here again, as in previous profiles, the trick is to circumvent those portions of the tool that expect input screens rather than input messages. Fortunately, significant future CASE development, as well as the structure of the AD/Cycle Information Model itself, assumes business logic input from messages, not screens. This will ensure more direct application of these tools in future message-based applications.

---

### CASE-GENERATED TRANSACTIONS AT A GLANCE

#### Use This Profile for . . .

Large-scale software development for business-oriented transactions.

#### Skill-Sets Required

1. Training in the selected CASE tool.
2. As much hands-on experience with CASE projects as possible.
3. Experience in building Distributed Function back ends.

#### Characteristics

+ **Higher productivity and quality:**
  CASE tools, which express business problems in higher-level constructs than COBOL, can significantly improve productivity and quality. This is especially true with an experienced team leader in charge.

+ **CASE tools are easily adapted to capsule transactions:**
  The simple structure of the capsule transaction can be easily accommodated by many CASE tools that can generate code.

− **Beware of using the tools beyond their capabilities:**
  You may be tempted to aim these tools at UI issues. If you want to build OOUIs, CASE is not the right tool for the job.

# 18

## *Profiles: Distributed Function Front Ends*

The profiles here take up the possibilities for the front ends of message-based, Distributed Function systems. Mixing and matching these front ends with last chapter's back ends yields many good possibilities for distributing application function across platforms.

The front-end profiles are:

- Programming to the UI API.
- Uni-GUI APIs.
- UI builders.
- Nonprogrammable terminal front ends.

### Front and Back Ends

Up to this point, we have talked about "front ends" and "back ends" simply as relative positions, but now it becomes necessary to be more precise. In front and in back of what? The industry tends to use the terms "front end" and "back end" to indicate a general orientation toward either the user or the database. The Trust Line demarcates one set of front and back, the communications wire another. In some contexts, the front end is the object region and the back end is the traditional function region.

For distinguishing between the two parts of a Distributed Function model, we will use this definition:

> Front end meets back end at the input port of the most downstream function dispatcher.

This line frequently coincides with the Trust Line, but it is not the same. The Trust Line separates platforms that can be trusted with community resources from those that can't, while the downstream-function-dispatcher line separates the user interface domain from the application programming domain.

### Front-End Roles

The front end (in the profile sense) of a system has these jobs:

- Provide the user interface.
- Perform data manipulation and integration functions.
- Form a message or set of messages to do the application's work.
- Send this message up to the function dispatcher.

All front-end profiles acknowledge the user interface, data manipulation, and message-forming jobs as their basic mandate. The fourth task, the actual hooking up of front end to back end via messages, is more problematic. Not all front ends can send messages in a way that the back end can understand. Some do not even accept this as part of their job, and they bow out once they have got the messages formed. Completing the connection between front end and back end, and making sure that the pieces actually fit together once they meet, could fall to you.

### Connecting Front End to Back End

Connecting a front end to a back end is essentially a plumbing job. Like a plumber faced with pipes of different diameters and even different threading, you may need special adapter fittings. Unlike a plumber, you will have to craft these adapters yourself.

First, settle upon a common protocol. Which protocol you choose will depend on (1) whether the front and back ends meet within the same machine, in which case you will choose among DLL, a named pipe, Dynamic Data Exchange, or the windowing system's base messaging protocol (e.g., PM messages), or (2) whether they are on remote machines, in which case you will choose a named pipe, LU6.2, TCP/IP, a LAN-specific protocol like Netbios, or any of a number of others. Company policy, the machines and skills available, and other factors will also affect your protocol choice.

If both front end and back end support the protocol of choice, you are home free. Very likely they won't. If there is a mismatch between what front end and back end will support, or if neither supports the protocol of choice, you will need to have an adapter built.

Building adapters is not easy. You will almost certainly need someone experienced with the protocols already in place on each side and with the linking protocol if it is different. (Not only do different protocols move data differently, they also have different ideas of the very structure of a communications event.) Still, as long as the adapter will play a limited role, such as facilitating simple request-reply interactions, a good implementer should be able to craft something quite serviceable.

On the bright side, adapters are completely generic and can move from program to program. If you have built a named pipe to LU6.2 adapter, pull it out any time you face a situation where these two protocols have to be linked.

## THE LONG-RUNNING-TASK PROBLEM

OS/2 and Windows programmers face an additional front-end to back-end interface hurdle. This is the infamous "long-running-task" problem. Certain windowing systems, such as OS/2 PM and Windows-16 bit (e.g., Windows 3), cannot tolerate an interruption of more than a fraction of a second in their message processing (one-tenth of a second is a good rule of thumb). If a PM program calls any function that exceeds this time limit, PM could freeze while waiting for the response. This type of behavior might be expected in Windows, since DOS can't really multitask, but it is quite disappointing in a system like OS/2 which has the facilities to do better. (The problem does not occur in Motif or Windows-NT.)

The long-running-task problem plagues cooperative processing applications more than most applications. PM will frequently need to pass a message to the back end and wait several seconds for a response. You do not want to risk freezing PM or, worse, crashing the system in the event that a line has dropped.

Fortunately, there is a relatively straightforward solution to this ugly problem. Make sure that a call to a long-running-task sends the message off to the task and returns immediately without waiting for the result. When the task completes, it can notify the PM application with a completion message. PM will stay happy, and the user can keep active while the long-running-task works away.

Some of the front-end profiles build this immediate-return mechanism into their products. For example, CICS/OS2's external call interface handles the back-end side of this problem, and Smalltalk's dual-threaded architecture handles it behind the scenes. But applications written directly in C or COBOL will have to resort to the technique described above.

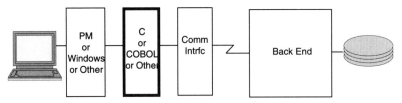

**Figure 18-1.**   *Profile: UI API*

## PROFILE: PROGRAMMING TO THE UI API

Most first-generation cooperative processing programs use this profile for their front ends. The developer employs a conventional programming language like C or COBOL and builds a user interface by invoking the API for the workstation windowing environment (Figure 18-1). (We usually designate the language/windowing pair with a "/". Thus, C/PM means a C program to the PM API; COBOL/WINDOWS means a COBOL program written on Windows.)

The popularity of this profile stems not from any inherent attractiveness, but from the lack of alternatives (now changing rapidly). This is very difficult programming. Project managers now expect that an experienced programmer who already knows the language will take 3–6 months to learn how to apply that language to building UIs. The programmer faces, after all, voluminous APIs with hundreds of functions, manually programmed event-driven structures, and an immature UI technology. Also, the different windowing environments vary dramatically in syntax and semantics, making the code extremely nonportable.

Despite all these drawbacks, programming directly to the UI API has its place. It is a good option for exploiting the full capabilities of the UI. If you want to invent a new type of control—for example, a circular scrollbar, a dial, or a voting-booth lever—UI API is a reasonable way to go. Programming to the UI API is like UI assembler: it is good for special tasks, you will be glad to have someone around who can do it, but you sure don't want to write applications this way.

### UI API AT A GLANCE

**Use This Profile for . . .**

Building specialized graphical elements only.

### Skill-Sets Required

1. Detailed knowledge of large UI APIs.
2. Familiarity with event-driven paradigm.
3. Master programmer to build the interface adapter.

### Characteristics

+ **Programming to the UI API is powerful:**
  Lets you do anything that the UI can do.

− **Difficult to program:**
  Expect long training times, long implementation schedules, and unpredictable results.

+ **Good for specialized UI implementation:**
  As with writing in assembler, it would be worthwhile to have a small group who can use UI API to build new graphical objects, controls, and viewers. It can provide these components to application programmers who are using other profiles.

− **Resulting programs are very nonportable:**
  UI APIs are so different from one another in both syntax and semantics that converting a program from one environment to another takes hard work. The "GUI wars" in the industry make this problem even worse. Application developers do not want to have to bet on which API will win.

0 **You're on your own with communications:**
  Any communications interface to the back end will need to be explicitly programmed. Remember to tend to the long-running-task problem.

## PROFILE: UNI-GUI APIS

Necessity being the mother of invention, vendors have jumped into the market with software libraries that sit on top of various windowing environments and purport to solve their incompatibility problems. We call these products "uni-GUI" APIs (Figure 18-2).

These products implement a set of function calls that perform the standard windowing operations and then turn around and call the host UI environment to satisfy the function. Structurally, the programs look like UI API programs in that they need to follow the same event-handling paradigm as the underlying UIs do. The value of a uni-GUI is not simplicity, but portability.

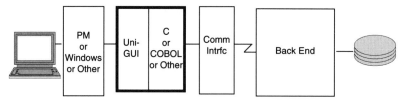

**Figure 18-2.** *Profile: Uni-GUI API*

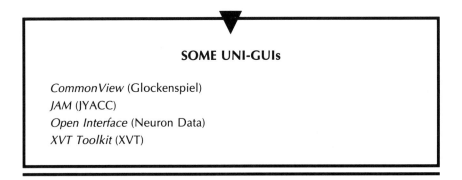

Unfortunately for this profile, UI environments are far richer than any uni-GUI can mask. Programmers describe "hitting the wall" when they need to address a UI feature that the uni-GUI won't let them reach. For example, if you want a PM retain-mode graphic to spin on the screen, plan to write this portion directly in the PM API. Such special programming can be kept to a minimum in most applications, and you can isolate it to increase portability. If you are determined to write UIs with a programming language, use a uni-GUI.

**UNI-GUI AT A GLANCE**

**Use This Profile for . . .**

Low-level construction of graphical interfaces with some degree of portability.

### Skill-Sets Required

1. Detailed knowledge of uni-GUI API.
2. Knowledge of native API where uni-GUI gives up.
3. Familiarity with event-driven paradigm.
4. Master programmer to build the interface adapter.

### Characteristics

+ **Applications reasonably portable:**
  You will be able to escape the main battles of the UI wars, but expect some border conflicts.

− **As hard to program as the UI API:**
  A uni-GUI does not make the job any easier, but you get more useful life out of the result. Since you have to worry about writing some portions of the code directly to the UI, this code may be harder to write, debug, and maintain than if you stuck with the UI.

− **Not as flexible as the native API:**
  Uni-GUIs do not let programmers get to all of the underlying functionality.

0 **You're on your own with communications:**
  Any communications interface to the back end must be explicitly programmed. Remember to tend to the long-running-task problem.

## PROFILE: UI BUILDERS

Dozens of tools in the marketplace build graphical user interfaces. Virtually all of them let you do the job in a fraction of the time that it would take to program a UI in one of the preceding profiles. Some are even commercial-grade enough for building industrial-strength applications (Figure 18-3).

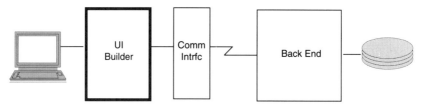

**Figure 18-3.** *Profile: UI builder*

▼

## SOME UI BUILDERS

*Toolbook* (Asymmetrix)
*ObjectVision* (Borland)
*Smalltalk* (Digitalk)
*Easel* (Easel Corp.)
*C++/CommonView* (Glockenspiel)
*Choreographer* (GUIdance)
*Level5 Object* (Information Builders)
*Enfin/2* (Software Productivity, Inc.)

Two of these products have been incorporated as strategic components in the AD/Cycle Generator box: Easel and Digitalk Smalltalk. Easel has been marketed primarily as a screen-scraper, but in fact it is a generic UI builder. Its event-driven language has been used to build many CUA Graphical Model applications. Digitalk is a more recent IBM partner. While it does not have, at the time we are writing, as well integrated a set of communication and database services as Easel, it is a fully object-oriented environment that has been used by the SAA CUA architects to prototype the CUA Workplace Model.

Overall, the market for UI builders is so volatile that the relative capabilities of competing products change every few months. We include a set of evaluation criteria for UI builders so that you can make a preliminary choice, but all tools will be evolving rapidly over the next few years. Do not let this volatility paralyze you. Build your front end in the most stable and capable UI builder you can find, and see what happens. Your decision about a UI is not irrevocable; your investment in time and money on the front end is not that great. Changing to another technology will be relatively cheap, especially relative to changing technology on the back end, which could entail astronomical costs. The front end is the least of your concerns.

### Evaluating UI Builders

When shopping for a UI builder, consider these factors (some are identical to screen-scraper criteria):

- **What user interface environment does it support?**
You will want portability among the important UI environments in order to keep your options open as industry directions change.

- **Is it object-oriented?**
When it comes to building GUIs and OOUIs, the more object-oriented a product is, the more you can expect to use it in the applications of the future. Evaluating a product's level of object support is tricky. All UI builders claim that they are object-oriented, and to some extent they are. It's the nature of the beast. GUI components themselves, like windows and controls, encapsulate state and behavior, and so they are themselves objects. The less-OO tools, like Toolbook, have objects on the fringes. Real OO tools, however, go much further, letting you carry the object paradigm way back into the application. So ask: Does the product provide a class library to develop with? Does the product allow for defining new classes? Does it support inheritance? If it does, you've got a true OO environment.

- **How does it interface with other system components?**
The UI builder will have to talk to the back end somehow, either via one of the local interface techniques mentioned above or through communications. You will want to know which local interfaces a product supports: DLL, DDE, PM messaging, named pipes. Find out if you will have to worry about the long-running-task with this product (someone who has already used it for cooperative processing can give you the straight scoop).

- **Does it have links to database and communications?**
The better choices will boast built-in capabilities or class libraries that support commercial communications like LU6.2 and linkages to relational databases. These products will save you having to build adapters, so you can get to work building cooperative processing applications that much quicker.

- **Does it support team development?**
This is an often-neglected line of inquiry. Eventually you will have a team of people working on this product. Effective team development requires features like version control, team access, and change control. Do not hamper your programming team with tools that won't allow sharing.

- **Is it proprietary?**
A fundamental question: Is this a one-of-a-kind development environment? Is the underlying language offered by anyone else or is it unique to this product? Even a very good proprietary solution could present long-term problems if the supplier disappears. To be

safe, choose a strategic front-end tool from a product set like C++ or Smalltalk where multiple vendors supply essentially standard products.

- **Is it flexible and powerful?**
  You will want a UI builder that gives you the full power of the native interface, not one that limits what you can do.

▼

---

**UI BUILDERS AT A GLANCE**

**Use This Profile for . . .**

Building powerful UI applications.

**Skill-Sets Required**

1. Training in the tool of choice.
2. Master programmer to build the interface adapter.

**Characteristics**

+ **Much more powerful environment for UI development:**
  Good tools will give order-of-magnitude improvements over conventional programming. The resulting code will be less convoluted and easier to maintain.

+ **Portable to multiple UIs:**
  This profile shelters developers from the worst fallout of the GUI wars and lets them support multiple versions far more inexpensively.

− **The tool set is changing rapidly:**
  Some tool vendors will go out of business, and new ones will appear. There will be rapid changes in which tools are the best ones. Cooperative processing developers should try to insulate themselves from these changes as much as possible.

0 **Some may not be as flexible as the underlying API:**
  Higher-level tools can sometimes block the developer from getting access to the full power of the user interface.

---

**PROFILE: NONPROGRAMMABLE TERMINAL FRONT END**

Dumb terminals, widely pronounced dead and buried, now arise to haunt a book on cooperative processing!

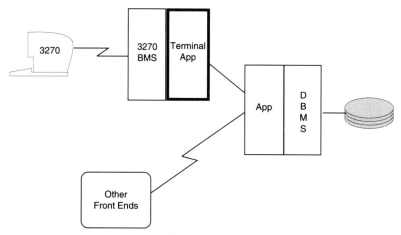

**Figure 18-4.** *Profile: Nonprogrammable terminal front end*

Actually, reports of their death have been greatly exaggerated. There are millions of dumb terminals (10 million 3270s alone) still chugging along. A significant number of sites will continue to use them for some time. Fortunately, accommodating them within a cooperative processing context is not hard (Figure 18-4). Once you have done the work of building a message-based back end, you have the interesting opportunity to "dual-port" its input. In other words, messages can come from an adjacent terminal transaction as well as from a remote workstation. Thus, the same application code can service both terminal and workstation, providing an excellent application-migration vehicle from terminals to workstations as they are installed.

---

## NONPROGRAMMABLE TERMINAL FRONT END AT A GLANCE

### Use This Profile for . . .

Building old-style terminal applications on the new Distributed Function application base—great for migration.

### Skill-Sets Required

1. Training on how to separate presentation from logic.

### Characteristics

−       **Not up to UI quality:**
        Of course, terminals cannot come close to providing the beauty, power, or intelligence of even the most primitive workstation interface. Use this profile only until better front-end machines are in place.

+       **Same application code serves both terminal and workstation:**
        Migration, rather than a forced march, is the best way for an organization to move toward cooperative processing. New application code can do double duty during the transition.

## WHERE TO SPEND YOUR MONEY

Over the last few years, we have become convinced that the most important step an organization can take toward cooperative processing is not to acquire and program workstations, but to rethink the design of its mainframe applications. If resources are limited, getting your mainframe architecture arranged properly is much more important than bringing workstations in house to work (even cooperatively) on poorly architected applications. Ordering hundreds of new workstations will please employees and make your company look progressive. But you would be much better off investing in good design and architecture, even if this means living with terminals for a few years longer.

# 19

# *Profiles: Object-Oriented Front Ends*

These final profiles concern the extreme front ends of systems. We are addressing them last because they differ in fundamental ways from other profiles. Instead of supporting one of the application models in Chapter 11, they build instead upon concepts in Chapter 14, "Distributed Design and Objects."

Both profiles here support the full CUA Workplace Model object-oriented user interface. Both use OO techniques throughout. Neither should be undertaken without a solid base of experience in OO programming. The two OO front-end components in this chapter are:

- The OO workplace.
- Formsets.

The first of these profiles describes the CUA Workplace Model in a bit more detail; the second introduces a specialized workplace object for transaction processing applications.

As we write this, there is almost no official tool support for OO workplace constructs, so both of these profiles require a "build or find-the-parts" mentality. Many organizations will choose to wait until full implementations or better tools are available. Others might want to forge ahead. For example:

- Some strategic applications will need the OOUI boost sooner. This has certainly been true in the software vendor community.
- Developers who are interested in these techniques for the future need to know *now* what OO front ends will look like so that they can build today's back ends in such a way that they will link up in the future.

- People sold on the power of OO interfaces will want them as soon as possible. For many applications, a cost-benefit calculation may support a decision to build now rather than buy later. Once the OOUI infrastructure is in place, building OOUIs turns out to be considerably easier and cheaper than building GUIs is today.

For the benefit of those organizations who have some OO experience in house and who decide to go ahead and take on one or both of these workplace profiles, we offer assorted nuggets of critical development information.

## PROFILE: OO WORKPLACE

OOUIs differ from other computerized user interfaces in a remarkable way. In traditional user interfaces, the developer's world and the user's world are described in completely different terms. For example, order-entry forms are programmed by screen maps. In an OOUI, the screen shows exactly the same objects that the developer created behind the scenes; the objects are projected onto the glass as if backlit.

### The User Looks at Objects

Take a moment to refamiliarize yourself with "An OOUI Demo" near the end of Chapter 9. The user sees and manipulates icon/objects such as an "inbox," "trash can," or "printer." Like every object, each of these icons has "state" and "behavior." The inbox's state includes whatever mail it contains; its "behavior" lies in how it responds to actions performed on it with a keyboard or a mouse, or its response to another object dropping down on top of it. Objects are often opened up and viewed through windows. Think of a window as a viewer, filter, or magnifying glass laid on top of an object to display its contents in a certain way. An object—say a set of data—can be viewed via several filters in several different windows simultaneously, perhaps as a spreadsheet and a card file. A change

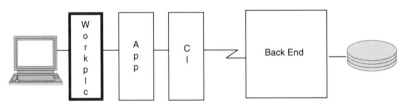

**Figure 19-1.**  *Profile: OO workplace*

to the data in any of the windows automatically affects the underlying data and any other window's rendition of it.

Notice also that every window contains at its upper left-hand corner a **title-bar icon**—a miniature version of the icon it is rendering. This surrogate icon lets a user manipulate the open window the same way she would manipulate the closed icon, and with the same results. She does not have to search around blindly for the antecedent icon that the open window may have covered up.

The most characteristic Workplace Model capability, drag-and-drop, encourages experimenting with object combinations. As the user drags an icon around the screen, he gets continual feedback from the objects whose airspace he is flying over. For example, if he attempts to drop an icon onto (or even just passes over) another object with which it has no possible interaction, the mouse pointer changes temporarily to a "No drop" signal.

### Buying or Building a CUA Workplace

The above description touches on the minimum set of behavior features that an OO workplace (Figure 19-1) must support. To summarize, these features are:

- Icons that behave as objects.
- Windows to view the objects.
- Title-bar icon.
- Drag-and-drop support.

By the time this book is published, you should be able to find these features in at least a few places:

- OS/2 Version 2 supports a workplace shell for interacting with the operating system. The API for this shell, currently unpublished, will be made available. This support will still require a considerable amount of programming.
- Digitalk Smalltalk currently supports all the functionality to build a workplace. It will be extended to support completed workplace classes.
- SPI's Enfin/2 supports workplace elements in their current version.

In addition, IBM has published several "red books" (see "Cooperative Processing Bibliography") that contain sample Smalltalk code for building workplaces.

▼

## OO WORKPLACE AT A GLANCE

### Use This Profile for . . .

Standardizing on the CUA Workplace Model.

### Skill-Sets required

1. Familiarity with CUA Workplace Model specifications.
2. Object-oriented programming to build and extend desktop.

### Characteristics

+ **Most powerful user interface architecture available:**
  The workplace classes open up full access to the CUA Workplace Model.

+ **Industry moving in this direction:**
  The SAA CUA priorities strongly promote the Workplace Model. Expect considerable tool support for and training in building and using these applications.

+ **Ease of creating new workplace objects:**
  Once basic workplace support becomes available, creating new application objects is simple.

− **Lack of commercially available workplaces:**
  This is still a build-it-yourself technology, though OO desktop classes will be available imminently. Workplace classes need to be built in a full OO environment.

− **Lack of workplace support in existing operating systems:**
  Ideally, the workplace classes should be available in the base operating system, rather than provided by third-party vendors or built by application developers. Without operating system support or universal API standards, it will be hard to get workplace objects from different development teams to work with each other.

---

### PROFILE: FORMSETS

For all the power of the Workplace Model, it is far from ready for widespread use. Since OOUIs grew out of the word processing/desktop-publishing world of individual users rather than the transaction-oriented world of businesses, they lack built-in objects that model complex commercial processes. The CUA Workplace Model comes with a plethora of generic desktop-type objects, as we have seen, but no higher-level, business-oriented objects.

Formsets (Figure 19-2) go a long way toward taking up the slack. The concept grew out of work done by a group of CUA architects and beta testers starting in 1989. Basically, formsets are high-level user interface

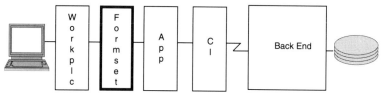

**Figure 19-2.** *Profile: Formsets*

controls that can simulate virtually any kind of business documents: order-entry forms, time cards, employee files, ship-docking manifests, tax returns, patient records. (In the first commercial appearance of a formset, in a cooperative processing human resource system developed by Tesseract Corporation, the formset implements documents for personnel, payroll, and benefits.)

A formset improves on a conventional form system in several ways:

- A formset does more than just receive data. It creates, maintains, and handles a simple or complex document throughout its entire life cycle. This means that it contains, in addition to the actual data entered, knowledge about the state of the work in progress: how much of it has been filled out, whose approval has been given and whose is still needed, whether there are any error messages pending, whether notes have been affixed in the course of the review process, and so on.

- A formset handles documents of any length, even complex, multi-page documents with optional attachments and exhibits.

- A formset assumes responsibility for the substantial form navigation logic that a complex document set requires. In older systems, this logic is built into the application, entangled with the transaction processing logic. A formset bundles this logic with the presentation piece instead, so that the back end is left with only business logic and database access. (This makes a formset a perfect match with the capsule back end, which does only the transaction piece and no form navigation at all.)

## Formsets in Action

Hydra's VIDOR application, described in Chapter 2, makes frequent use of formsets.

A video store clerk has opened the VIDOR workarea (Figure 19-3), which is where objects used for order processing are stored. He sees a pad of blank order forms labeled "Blank Formset," stickum notes, some pending documents, a returned formset, and two output bins.

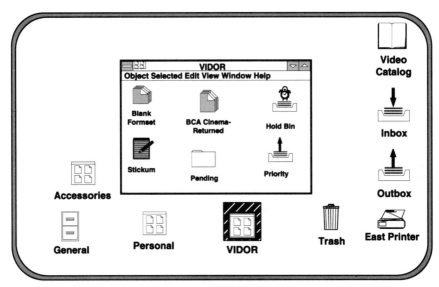

**Figure 19-3.** *Open the VIDOR workplace*

In Figure 19-4, he "tears off" an order form so that he can fill it out. As in the real world, he could also have filled out the order form (completely or only partially) while it was still attached to the pad and torn it off later.

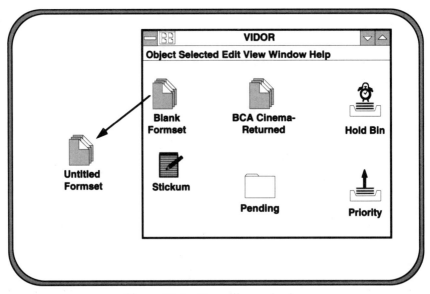

**Figure 19-4.** *Tear off an order form*

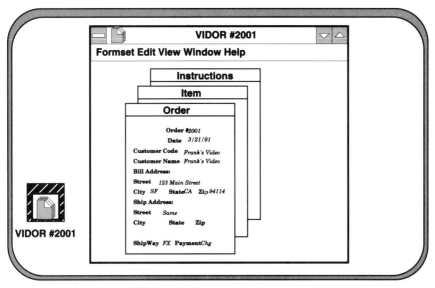

**Figure 19-5.** *Open the formset*

Now he double-clicks on the formset icon to open it (Figure 19-5). The formset contains three forms: an order header form, a repeating item form, and an optional instructions form. He starts filling it out. Note that the formset object title (below the icon) becomes the order number.

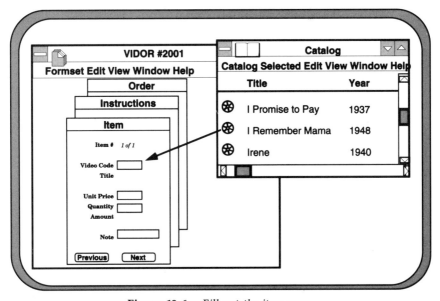

**Figure 19-6.** *Fill out the item page*

In Figure 19-6, he has started filling out the item form. He wants six copies of *I Remember Mama* and six copies of *Peeping Tom*. He selects the icons for these two films from the catalog, drags them to the item form, and drops them there. This operation "drains" the corresponding fields (video code and unit price) into the item form.

When he has finished filling out the order, he submits the formset. In Figure 19-7, he grabs the title-bar icon that sits right next to the system icon, drags it, and drops it on one of the output bins. This particular output bin is called "Hold Bin"; it collects formsets for subsequent processing (at a time the user can set with the alarm clock), whereas the "Priority Bin" submits them immediately. In either case, the output bin first sends a message back to the formset telling it to conduct any final cross-form semantic data checking, then render itself in output message form, and finally return this message to the bin.

This particular activity might have ended here, but a while later our customer finds some mail in his inbox (Figure 19-8). The formset has been returned with an Errors window noting that the store is over its credit limit and asking him to discuss the matter with his local customer service agent.

In Figures 19-9, 19-10, and 19-11, he opens up a stickum note, writes a message to his customer service rep at Hydra pointing out that he paid off his credit balance last week. He glues the stickum note to the formset and mails it off. Hearing nothing back, he can wait to receive his order and his invoice by mail.

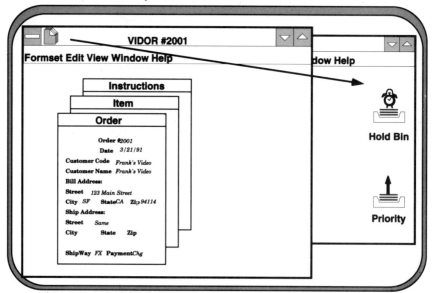

**Figure 19-7.** *Submit the transaction*

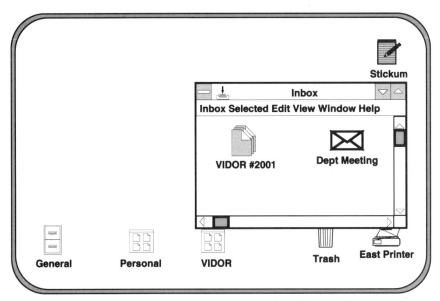

**Figure 19-8.** *Some time later . . . incoming mail*

Note a couple of things about this formset process. It simulates, but improves upon, "paper" catalog browsing, order processing, and dispute resolution. It also improves upon any conceivable terminal or even workstation transaction-processing system by handling with ease some

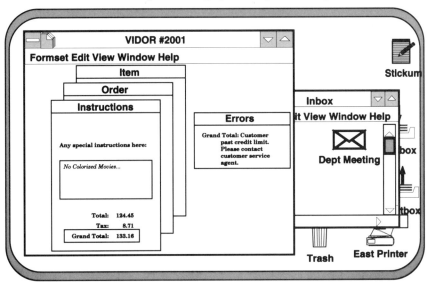

**Figure 19-9.** *Handle errors*

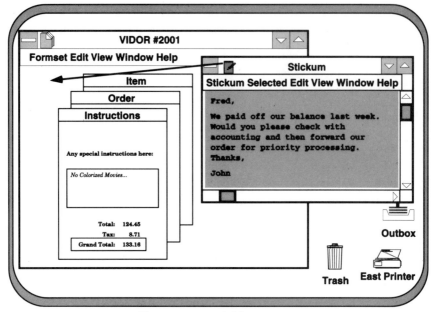

**Figure 19-10.**  *Stick on a note*

very difficult activities, such as ''pending'' a transaction in process, referring it to a user up the line, and attaching notes and comments.

Since every business handles bundles of forms at some point in its daily routine, the formset implementation is invaluable. Once in place,

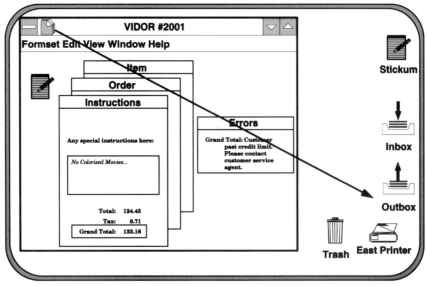

**Figure 19-11.**  *Send message to Hydra rep*

it will handle the user interface end of perhaps 80% of all business transactions.

### Programming Formsets

By the time this book appears, there may well be some vendor support for formsets in object-oriented UI builders. If not, you can build them from scratch or extend commercially available form systems to support formsets. The actual implementation is beyond the scope of this book (it will be "left as an exercise to the reader," as college textbooks put it), but here are a few important guidelines. These basic lessons come from our experience building formsets in Smalltalk.

- The high-leverage approach is to build a formset engine that can be "trained" to support different document sets. You cannot conceivably build a strong formset engine in anything but a pure OO environment.

- Once the formset engine is built, you need to hand it some information that tells it how to handle an instance of the formset. That information includes the following: an entity-relationship diagram that shows the hierarchy and cardinality of the forms in the formset (e.g., Order Form contains one-to-many Item Forms with an optional Instructions Form); a form definition for each; a field dictionary giving basic field names, types, and editing; and a description of the message format to unload the formset to.

- Formsets handle the vast majority of business documents that they have been tried on. Since they are programmed by *specification* only, you don't need to write programs for each new business document. In time, CASE tools that generate the back-end capsule transactions could also generate the formsets that drive them.

Formsets usually appear as a Distributed Function front end. Thus, our example shows the user filling out an order form and submitting it, causing a NewOrder message to be sent to the back end. But there is no reason this sequence could not be initiated and controlled by the host as well. The very same formset object could then be used for Distributed Presentation (in particular, the Distributed Dialog split described in Chapter 11). Such host-controlled dialogs have a variety of uses, including log-on and security sequences; system configuration; or, more generally, unanticipated or infrequently used dialogs. Host-controlled formsets keep the user's desktop from being cluttered with once-a-year dialogs. They also support high-priority *modal* dialogs (dialogs that the user must fill out before doing anything else) such as a password change.

▼

## FORMSETS AT A GLANCE

### Use This Profile for . . .

Building Workplace Model transaction-oriented applications.

### Skill-sets required

1. Object-oriented programming to build formset classes.
2. System analyst skills to define formset documents.

### Characteristics

+ **User sees transactions as objects:**
  Formsets bring OOUI power to transaction processing. Once documents are thought of as objects, they can be manipulated like any desktop object—they can be stored, mailed, deferred, routed, or submitted. The user learns to manipulate formsets as she would stapled business document sets.

+ **Application development is greatly simplified:**
  Once the basic formset machinery is created, a nonprogrammer can easily create document sets. These formset definitions do all the front-end work necessary to edit, maintain, and deliver a formatted message to the back end for processing.

− **Generic formset products are not yet available:**
  While we expect to see formsets available as general tools in some OO systems, they are not there at time of writing. Application developers need to consider whether it's worthwhile to build formsets themselves.

# 20

# *A System Built from Profiles*

Implementation profiles are, at last, the concrete building blocks of an application. Selecting the profiles best suited to your application's purposes, purchasing and/or building them, and then linking them together into an end-to-end system is where *Building Cooperative Processing Applications* actually begins.

This chapter takes you on a dry run in system design and profile assembly. It describes a sample session from the viewpoints of both user (left-hand column) and system (right-hand column), to serve as a kind of after-the-fact specification. The user activities start at the same point as the formsets description in the previous chapter, but the emphasis here is on how the system responds. You can follow the system actions by referring to Figure 20-1. Later we look under the hood at how the various strands of the application were implemented.

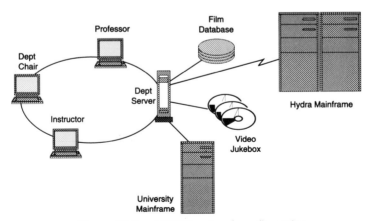

**Figure 20-1.** *VIDOR network configuration*

## Specification: VIDOR in Action

Hydra's VIDOR, the application described in Chapter 2, has now extended its reach out to the end user and broadened its range to incorporate catalog, research, and availability-check functions as well as simple ordering. To see how it works, we join college instructor Jeff Zorn putting together his new course on "Film Noir of the Fifties: The Existential Imperative."

Until recently, arranging a course like this required searching through multiple film catalogs, checking reference books for film credits and evaluations, renting tapes for preview purposes, phoning distributors to check on availability, scheduling meetings with colleagues, obtaining authorization from the department head, and filling out the university's standard purchase order in triplicate.

With the VIDOR system on his workstation, however, Zorn can do the job with dispatch. On his workstation screen is the now-familiar CUA Workplace Model, offering him a full range of office capabilities and a VIDOR workarea as well.

| User Viewpoint | System Viewpoint |
| --- | --- |
| Zorn's first task is to pick out eight classics of low-budget nihilism to show his class. He moves the mouse to the video catalog and double-clicks to open it and start his browsing. | Opening the video catalog accesses the Hydra movie database running on the English Department's LAN server. This database contains Hydra's extensively annotated film catalog. The database, originally used to facilitate the ordering process, has been enriched over the years so that it is now a valuable research tool as well. |
| The video catalog supports features for searching through the database. By pressing an onscreen "button" and filling out a form, Zorn sets data filters to help him narrow down his options. He successively chooses: Country (U.S.), Color (black & white), Year made (1950–1959), Running time (>100 minutes), Studio (all except MGM, 20th Century-Fox, and Paramount). To guarantee a pool of | Each filter automatically sends a SQL statement to the database to further limit a selection table. This table is then reaccessed by the workstation and redisplayed in the window. |

| User Viewpoint | System Viewpoint |
| --- | --- |

particularly disreputable films, he excludes any movie whose director, screenwriter, or stars have ever won an Academy Award. With each choice, the list of films in the catalog window shrinks.

The filtering process yields a list of 123 films, few enough to browse through. Zorn scrolls through the list. When a title catches his attention, he double-clicks on it. Detailed information on the movie pops up in a window: name of director, producer, screenwriter, actors, studio, a capsule summary, and quotes from reviews. There is also a "Preview" button that opens a video window and runs the movie's trailer on the computer screen.

A video request is routed to another network server devoted to supporting an "optical juke-box." This device loads the requested video disk, a CD-ROM, into a drive and accesses the relevant tracks. Video and audio data gets transferred back over the LAN and played on the workstation.

Zorn has decided to order *Kiss Me Deadly*. He "tears off" a blank order form with his mouse, opens it up so he can type into it, and fills out the basic ordering information.

This activity is all local to the workstation. It creates a new instance of the order form, monitors data entry, and checks for valid data. Some of the fields, like address and customer code, are filled in automatically.

Instead of typing in the name of the film, Zorn simply moves back to the video catalog window and "drags" the *Kiss Me Deadly* film reel to the order. All related order fields are automatically filled in.

This "drag-and-drop" on the workstation causes the video catalog window to hand over the data about the selected movie to the order-form application. At this point, the order form creates a CheckAvailability message and sends it in multiple directions. One copy goes to the university computer, which will check if anyone on campus already owns this movie, in which case Zorn will be notified by e-mail who the owner

| User Viewpoint | System Viewpoint |
|---|---|

| | is so he can inquire about borrowing it. Another copy of the Check-Availability message goes to the Hydra mainframe. The mainframe responds that the film is available for purchase. Had it been unavailable, a message box would have notified Zorn, and that film would have disappeared from the order form. |

Zorn selects and enters the rest of his movie selections. He now needs to run his choices by his department chair. He picks up the whole order form, drops it on the outbox icon, and sends it to her workstation.

The outbox e-mails a copy of the order-form formset object to the DeptChair, where it waits in her inbox for her examination.

She can review the order at her convenience. Should she be curious about any movie, she can double-click on the title to see the same information and preview that Zorn did.

When she's satisfied that the set of films will suit the needs of the department, she uses her mouse to tear off a purchase order number (PO #) request ticket and drag it over to the order form, where it sticks in place.

This action notifies the still terminal-based university purchasing system on the campus mainframe that the English Department is about to commit a certain amount of money. If this falls within the department budget, the mainframe responds with a PO #.

The next day, Zorn gets the order back with all selections approved and the PO # attached. He drops the completed order into the Submit box which will mail it off to Hydra.

The Submit box first notifies the order to prepare itself for transmittal. The order form makes sure that all its fields are completely filled out and does other final checks. When ready for transmittal, the order form is electronically

| User Viewpoint | System Viewpoint |
|---|---|

self-addressed. It goes to a communications gateway on the LAN where it is routed to the Hydra mainframe for processing.

At Hydra, the order-processing program checks the order for errors, verifies that the English Department's credit is good, accepts the order, and submits it to the system. It completes the transaction by sending an order confirmation back to the customer and routes the information on to an invoicing program.

Zorn's class sees the movies, gets depressed, and writes many ponderous papers that no computer can help Zorn read and grade.

## Designing the System

Figure 20-1 shows the configuration of the system described above. Each member of the English Department has a workstation. Each workstation runs a CUA Workplace environment, has access to a variety of individual and departmental applications, and can run formsets for university documents. The workstations are connected via **named pipes** to the LAN server, allowing for lightweight access to the server from both OS/2 and DOS workstations.

The LAN server supports the VIDOR video database, which the whole department shares. The LAN also includes an "optical jukebox" device that stores and plays CD-ROM optical disks. The server supports a direct connect to the university computer center and a phone communications link to remote electronic services, including the Hydra mainframe.

The VIDOR application that got Jeff Zorn his movies relies on a variety of application models and distribution models. (We ignore communication models because they tend to be very implementation-dependent and are often invisibly bundled into the available profiles.) Below is a summary of what each application strand does, what design model underlies it, and what implementation profile kicks in where.

### Handling User Actions

Application model: Local

Most basic user interface activity is handled locally on the workstation, including various **OOUI workplace** activities and **formsets**. Though these profiles operate locally at present, we expect that eventually the LAN server will act as a library for the hundreds of objects that populate a user community's desktops. These object databases will be accessed via client/server distribution and should be transparent to the local workstation applications.

### Browsing through the VIDOR Database

Application model: Distributed Data Access
Distribution model: Client/server

When a user at a workstation browses through or queries the movie database, the workstation uses a **distributed database front end** to provide a visual database query tool. As the user either picks prepackaged queries or forms *ad hoc* queries, the front end submits SQL SELECT statements to the LAN database, accessing various sets of data that are in turn displayed to the user.

A special operation lets Zorn drag the selected movie and drop it on the order form. The easiest way to implement this linkage is to "train" each of these objects (formset and front-end tool) to know about the other so that they can exchange specified information when one is dropped on the other. A richer alternative utilizes a technique we call "field draining." A field drain is like a COBOL MOVE CORRESPONDING. It moves like-named fields from one object to another, even if the objects have never met before. This is an effective technique for building multipurpose objects; as yet, however, there is little standards work in this area.

### Previewing a Movie

Application model: Distributed Function
Distribution model: Client/server

Pressing the Preview button while browsing through movies notifies a server process to transfer a *blob* (binary large object—possibly the movie trailer) from the optical jukebox to the workstation. An easy way to do this would be a client/server interaction (an RPC would be great here) to a **capsule transaction**. The LAN process may need to talk to both the database (to get location information) and the jukebox. Once it has been retrieved (30 seconds if the CD-ROM needs to be changed), the blob gets transferred back to the workstation.

### Checking Movie Availability

Application model: Distributed Function

Distribution model: Peer-to-peer

Checking movie availability calls for a complex application strand. When a movie title is entered into a formset, the formset emits a Check-Availability message to the nearest **function dispatcher**, which in this case lives on the workstation and ties to a cascade of upstream dispatchers on the LAN server and at Hydra headquarters. This message is passed up to the LAN server, which in turn routes messages to multiple peers to check on film availability. It maintains a "say-and-stay" (i.e., request-reply) with the Hydra host while a **capsule transaction** determines the film's availability. It also sends a "say-and-pray" (broadcast and hope someone responds) to the university computer, which will see if it can locate any copies already on campus.

### Getting the University PO #

Application model: Distribution Presentation

Getting a PO # assigned to the order form poses an interesting challenge, because the university's purchasing department has never updated its old 3270 system. Various departments, frustrated at having to support and teach two different interfaces, have installed **screen-scrapers** to renovate the displays of the more popular applications. When the department chair pulls a PO # request ticket off the workplace pad and drops it on an order, a screen-scraper behind the scenes executes a 3270 transaction that supplies the ordering department, order number, and purchase amount and receives back a PO # by way of authorization, which it sticks on the order form.

Notice that we assign no distribution model to screen-scraping. One could argue that it displays some attributes of client/server (user requests/system responds) and some attributes of peer-to-peer (ability to reverse the channel and send unanticipated messages). But, at heart, screen-scraping is simply a trick played on a data stream. A message stream that was never designed for process-to-process interactions should not be dignified with an architected title.

### Submitting the Order

Application model: Distributed Function
Distribution model: peer-to-peer

Finally, we consider the mainline activity of the application. When the order-form icon gets dropped on the Submit box, the workplace sends a message to the **formset** to check itself and then unload itself into a message. This message is passed to the workstation **function dispatcher**, which hands it up its cascade until it hits Hydra. Here the message finds a matching **capsule** transaction that processes the order. Since inbound transactions are coming from customers, all are treated as untrusted messages. This means that all edits, whether they were known to be done or not, are repeated. The basic order-form edits are redone, the film availability is confirmed (perhaps the stock has been depleted since Zorn requested the film), and the credit limit is again checked (perhaps there's been a flurry of orders from Zorn's department). It may seem a heavy burden to place on the system, but it allows maximum flexibility in the hands of the customer.

When the NewOrder transaction has been completed, Hydra sends a message back to its peer, Zorn's workstation, either acknowledging a successful order or informing the formset of errors.

The credit-checking, order-placing, and billing activities inside the capsule transaction rely on traditional programming that any experienced CICS programmer can do easily.

### The Peopleware (The People? Where?)

Like many of our profiles, the team behind such a multithreaded project is not something you can "buy off the shelf." You will have to assemble it yourself. Building cooperative processing applications calls for an odd combination of skills, a *Magnificent Seven*-type group, diverse and possibly contentious, under a determined leader.

- **Application builders:** This group handles the basic business programming—for VIDOR, principally writing the capsule transactions. In most environments, this group will be COBOL programmers or CASE tool users who know applications and how to talk to a database. They may have migrated from more conventional mainframe programming activities, and they will have had to forget most of what they know of talking to screens. The more advanced application builders will work with the system architect to define and implement the protocol of the function dispatchers and environmental scaffolding. If they follow the concepts in this book, these programmers can build applications to execute on the host, LAN server, and even the client.

- **Front-end builders:** This small group will build, from scratch or with the help of purchased products, the desktop, various viewers, and workstation-based application code to implement powerful front-end applications like the order form. They may know very little about the underlying application. They concentrate on providing tools for the application builders.

- **A network plumber:** A healthy cooperative processing project will need the services, at least part-time, of someone who knows how to glue different environments together. This may involve mastery of a variety of networking protocols such as named pipes, TCP/IP, OSI, LU6.2, or others. A well-designed system will require only a small amount of such plumbing, but a weaker design (one that overuses communications-aware transactions, for example) will probably need a communications specialist as a full member of the team.

- **The cooperative processing architect:** This is probably the hardest job to define, and it's certainly the hardest to staff. As long as cooperative processing systems have to be built in a split-paradigm environment, e.g., for the foreseeable future, success will depend on an architect who can envision the entire application end to end. This individual needs a true appreciation for—and, if possible, some background in—both workstation and host technology. He has to communicate with application builders, front-end builders, and network plumbers, and he must understand large chunks of what each group is doing. Probably the architect's main job is to mediate the "negotiated settlement" and to boil down the resulting agreement into a message protocol that both sides can work with as their specifications.

If it succeeds, the cooperative processing team will have done far more than design and build a new application. In getting people with diverse skills and backgrounds to pool their efforts, it will have served as a pilot project for bringing cooperation to processing. Ultimately, cooperative processing systems aim at recasting an organization's information systems, and possibly human systems as well, into a more integrated and effective effort than ever before.

# Cooperative Processing Bibliography

There is a great deal of reading material relating to the topics addressed in this book. Here are the books and articles that we think are the most useful.

## Systems Application Architecture and Related Topics

Grochow, Jerrold M. 1991. *SAA: A Guide to Implementing IBM's Systems Application Architecture.* Englewood Cliffs, N.J.: Yourdon Press.

Probably the best management-level book on SAA. It is quite evaluative and incorporates the insights of someone who has built a working SAA system.

Martin, James, with Chapman, Kathleen K., and Leben, J. 1991. *Systems Application Architecture: Common User Access.* Englewood Cliffs, N.J.: Prentice Hall.

A complete look at CUA, including some implementation issues under OS/2, Office Vision, and other environments. It seems especially targeted to lower-grade user interfaces (3270s) and offers little insight into object-oriented user interfaces.

Orfali, Robert, and Harkey, Dan. 1991. *Client-Server Programming with OS/2 Extended Edition.* New York: Van Nostrand Reinhold.

A sprawling book. While somewhat light on big-picture issues, a gold mine of tips, techniques, and trade secrets. Hundreds of pages of C source code, plus some extremely valuable benchmarks. Many Dialog Manager references, which should be ignored.

## Distributed Systems

Coulouris, George F., and Dollimore, Jean. 1988. *Distributed Systems: Concept and Design.* New York: Addison-Wesley.

An excellent book on the thorny issues surrounding distributed systems. Includes good definitions of client/server and processor pools. Whole chapters on distributed files, remote procedure calls, and distributed transaction services. A don't-be-without book.

Mullender, Sape, ed. 1989. *Distributed Systems.* New York: Addison-Wesley.

A collection of technical papers on all aspects of distributed computing. Especially good sections on distributed transaction processing by Alfred Spector (now of Transarc Corporation).

## Object-Orientation

Booch, Grady. 1991. *Object-Oriented Design with Applications.* Redwood City, Calif.: Benjamin/Cummings.

Written by one of the creators of OO design. A clearly written and erudite book. Describes the whole progression of OO thought from goals and principles all the way to sample applications in Smalltalk, C++, and others.

Coad, Peter, and Yourdon, Ed. 1990. *Object-Oriented Analysis.* Englewood Cliffs, N.J.: Yourdon Press.

Interesting; focuses specifically on the systems analysis phase and describes the conjunction of OO thought with entity-relationship diagrams. Despite some rather idiosyncratic ways of presenting ideas, discusses one of the more fruitful topics of the day: how to combine the new OO technology with existing methods and methodologies.

Cox, Brad, and Novobilski, Andrew. 1991. *Object-Oriented Programming: An Evolutionary Approach* (2d Edition). Reading, Mass.: Addison-Wesley.

By object-orientation pioneer Brad Cox. Details, among other things, his conviction that a software industrial revolution will lead to a software components industry.

Wirfs-Brock, Rebecca, Wilkerson, Brian, and Wiener, Lauren. 1990. *Designing Object-Oriented Software.* Englewood Cliffs, N.J.: Prentice-Hall.

A very readable book on OO design, with plenty of examples. Espouses "responsibility-driven" design which involves a methodical search for classes, for the responsibility each class owns, and for the collaborator classes required to satisfy the responsibility. This technique's principle CASE tool—a pack of 3x5 index cards!

## Information and Business

Keen, Peter G. W. 1991. *Shaping the Future: Business Design through Information Technology.* Cambridge: Harvard Business School Press.

Explores the value of information technology for a business's competitive health. Introduces author's "reach and range" analysis and applies it to several business cases.

## IBM Publications
(Entries are preceded by the IBM part number.)

SBOF-1240. The SAA Library.

Approximately twenty manuals that document the essential aspects of SAA and its interfaces.

G321-0091. *IBM Systems Journal* 27, no. 3, 1988.

A special issue on SAA. Some of the articles dated now and of primarily historical interest. Two particularly important articles: "Introduction to System Application Architecture" by Earl Wheeler and Alan Ganek—conveys the founder's vision of SAA; and "SAA Distributed Processing" by Alan Scherr—describes system splits we've come to call distributed application models.

G321-0099. *IBM Systems Journal* 29, no. 2, 1990.

> A special issue on AD/Cycle. Articles give a considerable amount of insight into the underpinnings of AD/Cycle, including strategy, role of process management, and Repository technology.

GG24-3295. *SAA and LU6.2 Considerations on CICS/MVS Applications.* ITSC ("Red Book"). 1989.

> The ITSC books are bright red, usually written very clearly (like cookbooks), and cost a few dollars. Worthwhile even for people not interested in CICS, MVS, or LU6.2. Details, with working code, the function dispatcher and capsule transaction concepts used in this book. Contains CICS-dependent scaffolding, but the dispatcher and transaction examples are highly portable.

GG24-3641. *A Practical Introduction to Object-Oriented Programming.* ITSC. 1990.

GG24-3580. *Developing a CUA Workplace Application.* ITSC. 1990.

ZZ81-0251. *Management Implications of Implementing SAA Workplace Applications.* ITSC. 1990.

ZZ81-0271. *Data Access in an Object-Oriented Environment.* ITSC. 1990.

GG24-3566. *Object-Oriented Analysis of the ITSO Common Scenario.* ITSC. 1990.

GG24-3647. *Object-Oriented Design a Preliminary Approach.* ITSC. 1990.

GG24-3581. *Managing the Development of Object-Oriented Applications.* ITSC. 1990.

> Set of red manuals that probably costs less than any commercially published computer book. Manuals contain a course-worth of material on OO development that works through the development of a few applications and comes with complete Smalltalk/V (Digitalk) source code for these applications. Inconceivable that anyone interested in cooperative workplace applications would be without these.

## Tibbetts/Bernstein: Important Articles on Cooperative Processing and SAA

June 15, 1991. SystemView Report Card. *Software Magazine.*

June 1991. Non-Cooperative Systems at IBM. *News 3X/400.* (Lays out relationship of cooperative processing and client/server.)

March 15, 1991. AD/Cycle Report Card. *Software Magazine.*

January 1991. Software Malls. *Software Magazine.* (Explores architecture of SAA Common Applications.)

November 1990. Is IBM Raising Hurdles Beyond Others' Reach? *Software Magazine.* (Explains DRDA and presents third-party reaction to it.)

September 1990. Discredited Dialogs. *SAA Update.* (Implications of not enhancing SAA Dialog Interface.)

June 1990. Why SAA Will Play on Local Area Networks. *Datamation.* (Not at all about what *Datamation* titled it! This is an essay on SAA evolution into the early nineties.)

June 1989. This Application SAA Certified. *SAA Update.* (Reflections on compliance and certification issues.)

March 1989. A Cooperative Primer. *SAA Age.* (The "power nozzle" comes to life again in this starter set for cooperative processing.)

# *Index*